PARENT
IN CONTROL

GREGORY BODENHAMER

A FIRESIDE BOOK
PUBLISHED BY SIMON & SCHUSTER

F

FIRESIDE

Rockefeller Center
1230 Avenue of the Americas
New York, NY 10020

FIRESIDE and colophon are registered trademarks
of Simon & Schuster Inc.

Designed by Irving Perkins Associates

Manufactured in the United States of America

3   5   7   9   10   8   6   4

Library of Congress Cataloging-in-Publication Data

Bodenhamer, Gregory.
    Parent in control / Gregory Bodenhamer.
        p.   cm.
    Includes bibliographical references and index.
    "A Fireside book."
    1. Parent and teenager.   2. Teenagers—Discipline.   3. Adolescent
psychology.   I. Title.
HQ799.15.B63   1995
649′.125—dc20   95-535
                                                                                      CIP

ISBN 0-684-80777-7

To my wife, Terrie,
and to the memory of my friends
Edgar Taylor and Shirley Lawther

AUTHOR'S NOTES

I apologize to those of you who will be offended by the use of rough and profane street language, but it is important to portray the real-life situations described in this book as accurately as possible. Unfortunately, many children use highly offensive language.

The people described in this book are real. Their names and identifying characteristics have been changed to protect their privacy.

CONTENTS

Introduction   13

1. The Kids Before Back in Control   17

2. Understanding Children's Misbehavior   23

3. Behavioral Templates   34

4. Rules   56

5. Provocation and Manipulation   62

6. Flawed Supervision: Parent Out of Control   76

7. How to Regain Control of Out-of-Control Children   101

8. Jason, Eddy, Julie, Bonita, and Nicole Revisited   133

9. The Success Continues   142

10. Parents in Control—At Last   155

Appendix: Questions and Answers   163
Bibliography   175
Index   177

For the things which we have to learn before we can do them we learn by doing: men become builders by building houses, and harpists by playing the harp. Similarly, we become just by the practice of just actions, self-controlled by exercising self-control, and courageous by performing acts of courage.

—ARISTOTLE, Nichomachean Ethics

INTRODUCTION

I have written this book for the frustrated, frazzled, and frequently overwhelmed parents, stepparents, parenting-again grandparents, and foster parents of the worst-behaved generation of children in American history. I have also written it for the educators, police, probation officers, and social workers who work with this generation of children.

Back in Control: How to Get Your Children to Behave

In the past twenty years there has been a continuing weakening of parental authority and a corresponding increase in the number of families with willful, incorrigible, and delinquent children—children who are tougher, meaner, and more aggressive than the children of ten or twenty years ago. These children bring chaos not only to their homes but to their schools and neighborhoods as well, and are determined to have their own way at all costs. They not only argue that black is white, but aggressively argue about the nature, texture, composition, and meaning of black and white, and about whether black and white even exist, and if they do exist who had them last ("It wasn't me!"). Some of them, though, are children who won't even bother to argue. They just do as they please as soon as their parents turn their backs or, in many instances, even if parents don't turn their backs. Additionally, these children frequently take on an "up yours" attitude that sorely tempts even gentle, passive parents toward child abuse or abandonment. They also make it clear that their friends and peers always come first, before everyone and everything else, especially family.

As far as specific misbehavior is concerned, this group of children also includes the kids who haven't done homework in months or years ("They don't give any" or "I did it in class"), the kids who know the local street cops better than they know their teachers, and the kids whose misbehavior causes parents to be on a first-name basis with school disciplinarians, social workers, psychologists, police, probation officers, and public defenders.

Most parents with out-of-control children have been everywhere and done everything to try to change their children's behavior, with little or no success. Not just a few have paid tens of thousands of dollars for hospital-based programs or for psychiatric or psychological counseling, only to find that counseling and therapy are usually ineffective in controlling willful, incorrigible, or delinquent behavior. They also find that those behavior changes that are gained in counseling and hospital programs don't last and, unfortunately, that some kids come out of these programs in worse condition than when they went in.

Parents of these difficult, hard-to-discipline children are also tired of unsupportive or hostile parenting professionals who clearly don't understand the problems involved in raising willful, incorrigible, or delinquent children or who undermine parental authority on purpose because they believe the use of parental authority is immoral.

Hundreds of thousands of desperate families have gone to parenting programs where they were told that parents don't have the ability or the right to control their children. Instead they were told to "release with love," or to give their children the "freedom to fail." And those parents who went ahead and released their children with love and actually gave them the freedom to fail usually found their children quickly mastering the art of failure. These families have also discovered, early on, that out-of-control children are usually willing to endure any punishment and the loss of any reward as long as they can get their own way. And they've found that punishments, rewards, contracting systems, and Tough Love approaches used by other parenting professionals are close to useless in restoring order in their homes.

Fortunately, however, unlike any other program or approach, the material presented in this book can help restore parental structure and authority to every family wishing to use it. In our parenting workshops at the Back in Control Center we have successfully worked with thousands of out-of-control, chaos-producing kids, including young burglars, car thieves, runaways, drug and alcohol abusers, and mother-beaters. We have worked with kids who won't talk and kids who won't shut up. We have also worked with sexually aggressive seven- and eight-year-olds and with the teenage mothers of AIDS babies. Many of the kids we have successfully returned to the structure of their families were members of incorrigible child-based criminal or racist subcultures including young "militiamen," skinheads, heavy metalers, punks, gothics, and other so-called alternative kids as well as inner-city gang members who were also shooters, robbers, and drug dealers.

Using the concepts in this book, most parents will be able to restore order in their homes within days or weeks. Others, depending on the tenacity and temperament of both children and parents, may need a Back in Control–trained parent-trainer or a probation officer, social worker, or therapist to help them implement the program. And families with violent teenagers, habitual runaways, or children regularly involved in crime may need to start with a well-designed, tightly supervised wilderness program or a highly disciplined, well-supervised residential treatment program to start the restructuring process that will continue at home. Families whose children are involved in crime may also need the support and authority of the juvenile court to help implement the program successfully. But virtually all children can be structured to be hardworking, organized, sober, honest, and honorable—as long as their parents and other adults with authority are willing to put in the time and energy needed to implement the concepts and methods set out below.

1

THE KIDS BEFORE
BACK IN CONTROL

Jason: The Gangster

Jason wasn't a big boy, but he had the personality of a pit bull. Anytime he didn't get his way he would badger those who opposed him until he wore them out. His father gave up trying to control Jason by the time he was six years old, but his mother, even though she was emotionally drained and physically worn down, continued the fight to keep Jason's chaos restrained for another ten years—until he became a violent gangster. He first hit his mother when he was sixteen and she was forty-four. It was on a school night when his mother told him to stay home and finish his studies.

His mother had just closed the front door, leaving one of his gangster friends on the porch. Jason and his mother were standing in the entryway, arguing. "No. You're not going out," she said firmly and grabbed his arm to keep him from leaving.

He wrenched his arm out of her grip, shoved her hard against the wall, and knocked the air out of her lungs. "Goddammit," he screamed, "leave me alone."

As Mom reached out to grab Jason's arm, he spun around, fist clenched, and hit her in the face. She fell to the floor, sobbing, and he walked out the front door.

He came back two hours later, just in time to hear two uniformed police officers tell Mom there was nothing they could do to help her. If her husband had battered her, they could take him to jail. If she

were twenty-five years older, and Jason had hit her, they could take
him to jail for elder abuse. And if she had hit him the way he hit her,
they certainly would take her to jail. But she was told that the
juvenile hall and juvenile court were so overcrowded that they had
been ordered not to bring kids in for beating up parents unless they
were bloodied or crippled by the assault.

For the next two months she did her best to keep Jason under
control as he continued to physically intimidate her, getting support
from no one until she enrolled in a Back in Control program.

Eddy: An Alcohol and Tobacco User

Eddy was a twelve-year-old alcohol abuser when his mother
brought him to a Back in Control Center in Southern California. He
was a strikingly good-looking little boy. He was bright, but failing
most of his subjects. He was charming much of the time, but was
always in trouble at school. He was the fastest, most athletic boy in
his school, faster as a sixth grader than anyone in the seventh or
eighth grade. But when he started hanging out with the street
toughs who went to his school, he dropped out of the youth soccer
and Little League programs in which he excelled and started smoking and drinking. His mother was afraid that he was becoming just
like his father.

Eddy's father had returned to his native Costa Rica three years
earlier and the family hadn't seen him since, which was fine with
Eddy's mother. She and Eddy no longer had to endure her ex-
husband's beatings, his anger, his drunkenness, and his womaniz-
ing. But for nine years, until the day he left, he had made sure his
little "macho man" understood that men never took orders from
women and that Eddy was to stand up to his mother and to any
other woman who tried to tell him what to do. The father also
thought it was cute when his son got drunk on the beer he gave
him. Three years after the father left, Eddy was still defying his
mother and his female teachers. At home he threw violent tantrums to get his way. His mother's arms and shins were covered
with bruises as a result of his violent attacks. He was also being
truant from school, hanging out and drinking with some of the

neighborhood's street toughs, and not coming home until late at night.

His mother was emotionally overwhelmed and feared that she might hurt or kill her son or that he would be taken away by the Los Angeles County Department of Children's Services because of her abuse. She had been in several different counseling programs with Eddy, but the therapists either made her feel she was a bad parent or that Eddy was a sociopath beyond redemption and beyond her ability to control. She was also referred to a twelve step program, Alanon, where she was told there was nothing she could do to stop her twelve-year-old son from drinking and that she should "release him with love."

Julie: A Runaway

Fourteen-year-old Julie was once a parent's delight. She was polite, well mannered, and helpful. She was warm and affectionate. She was a good student and was halfway decent about doing her chores. But that was in the past. Then she started looking and acting like one of those surly fourteen-year-olds seen on daytime television arrogantly telling everyone in the audience that she can handle childbirth, parenting, and whatever drugs she chooses to use and that no one is going to tell her otherwise.

The change was concurrent with her bonding with Sean, an unemployed nineteen-year-old high school dropout who demanded obedience from the girls and women in his life. From the day she met him at the Taco Bell down the street from her school—which had an open campus and an administration that made no effort to supervise its students during lunchtime—she started taking on his values, behaviors, attitudes, and character. That afternoon, when her mother asked her about school, as she had done each day from the beginning of kindergarten, Julie snapped, "That's my business," and walked to her room, where she spent the rest of the night. Nothing her parents said got her to tell them what was wrong.

Julie started sneaking out of the house at night, sometimes staying away for days at a time. She started cutting classes and then went to all-day truancies. She dropped out of her after-school sports programs, abandoned all of her old friends, and stopped playing her music. Her grades fell from the honor roll to the "at risk" list. All she wanted to do was be with Sean. Even after he started hitting her—she couldn't hide the bruises from her mother—and controlling every aspect of her life, including what clothes she was to wear, where she could go, and who she could be with, she wouldn't leave him, physically or emotionally. She would come home to get clean clothes, a good meal, and a hot shower; then she would run away to be with Sean again.

Both of the therapists that Julie's parents saw by themselves—Julie refused to go—said there was nothing the parents could do unless Julie wanted help. They tried to help them deal with and accept the loss of their fourteen-year-old daughter. When Julie's dad went to the police, he was told that they could do nothing about runaways and that unless Julie would testify against Sean, the prosecuting attorney couldn't charge him with statutory rape, despite her miscarriage. Their priest suggested that they pray for God's help.

Bonita: Sex in the Neighborhood

Until her father died and she and her mother moved to her grandmother's house in a blighted, deteriorating part of the city, Bonita had been a polite and well-behaved little girl. But Bonita soon developed an attitude problem and started challenging her mother about chores, schoolwork, and curfews, which her mother thought was normal for a ten-year-old. What caught her mother off guard was Bonita's introduction to sex at such an early age.

While sorting the family's wash, Mom found a pair of Bonita's panties streaked with blood. When asked about the panties, Bonita initially refused to answer. But after Mom had her disrobe and found that her genitals were raw and scratched, Bonita admitted that she and Tyler, an eleven-year-old neighborhood boy, had had sex in his bedroom the previous afternoon. She also admitted that she'd had sex with two other preteen boys in the previous three months—once at a girlfriend's home and once in a vacant apartment near the school. She told her mother that, from the day she had moved into that neighborhood, not only the boys but also the girls had pressured her into having sex. Day after day all of her friends had called her names—"mama's girl" and "baby girl"—and ridiculed her for being a virgin.

She cried in her mother's arms and told her how much her attempts at sex had hurt and how ashamed she felt. But she admitted that being ridiculed by her friends also hurt and that she wanted to be accepted. It was clear to Mom that Bonita was confused, frustrated, embarrassed, and unlikely to stand up to her friends on her own.

Nicole: School Problems

Nicole's problems started when she was in the first grade. She was the youngest student in her class, and no matter how hard she tried, no matter how much time she spent on the task, no matter how closely she paid attention to directions, Nicole couldn't print or draw as well or as fast as the other students in her class. Compounding the problem, her fine motor skills were slow to develop, and her teacher slow to understand the problem. Like many underachieving students, Nicole's early school experiences crippled her ability to learn. Beginning in that bad first year, she started developing and using defensive strategies to avoid the horrible feelings of defeat and failure that were her daily companions at school.

By the beginning of second grade, Nicole was so repelled by her experiences at school that she quit trying to be a student and took up clowning. Occasionally she would get an extraordinary teacher, as she did in fourth grade, who knew how to keep her focused for extended periods of time, but more often than not, she had teachers who quickly grew tired of the provocations and manipulations she used to get out of doing her assignments.

In middle school she developed friendships with other underachieving and turned-off students who reinforced and protected each other's already negative feelings toward school. And when it was time for her to graduate from the eighth grade, no adult in the school was sorry to see her or her coterie of clowns and misfits leave.

Her first year of high school was a disaster. Within a month she was failing, or close to failing, every subject. She refused to suit up for physical education. She wouldn't do her homework. She was disruptive and belligerent in the classroom. And she failed to show up for detention or Saturday school.

Her parents tried to help her. They bought a study program called *Where There Is a Will There Is an "A,"* and they found she had no will. They tried to pay her to earn good grades, but she never got grades good enough to pay. They grounded her, turned off the television, and cut off her use of the telephone, but she chose to be grounded and go without the telephone and television rather than study. They lectured her, sharing their experience and expertise, but she just argued with them. They took her to the counseling department at their HMO twice, and after both eight-session blocks—the maximum under their employer's health insurance contract—they were told that nothing could be done until Nicole wanted to change. They had the school district test her for possible placement in special education programs, but she was too intelligent and, despite her rebellion, had learned too much. Her parents were ready to give up.

2
UNDERSTANDING CHILDREN'S MISBEHAVIOR

§

Temperamentally Difficult Children

Not all children are easy to raise. Some, as even the best of parents have found out, test the extreme limits of parents' patience. And some push way beyond those limits. Worse yet, for everyone concerned, many are seemingly born to challenge the limits on virtually everything. Others, after learning how to manipulate, provoke, and otherwise control their parents, seemingly change in midstream from normal everyday kids to modern-day protégés of Mr. Hyde.

Temperament plays a large part in determining how people view the world and live their lives. Children at risk for life failures—dropping out of school, teenage pregnancy, chronic unemployment, drug and alcohol abuse, and crime—are frequently born with a combination of intense temperament traits that test the mettle of even the most loving and steadfast parents. Typically, in varying degrees, they are difficult, self-centered, and insensitive to the feelings of others. Many of them are also aggressive. Like a rope being pulled in a tug of war, there is an ever-present tension between adult-imposed rules and temperamentally difficult children's desires to do as they please. They act on impulse and desire—on what they feel like doing—not reason or logic. In fact, doing what they feel like doing at the moment is the most important goal in their lives. They use logic and reasoning only to figure out how to get their way or how to stay out of trouble in case they're caught, not to decide whether they should or shouldn't misbehave.

Even mature, logical adults sometimes have problems with impulse control and other emotionally based decisions. More than a few of us have looked at a freshly baked cinnamon roll or a hot slice of pizza, smelled its aroma, and been in an immediate internal fight between that part of the brain that controls logic ("No, no, don't do it") and the part that controls our impulses ("Eat it, eat it, eat it, eat it!"). Many of us all too often do eat it. Temperamentally difficult children, however, normally don't even bother to engage in the battle between reason and impulse. If they feel like eating the cake, they eat it, and then they use their logic and reasoning to make it look as if the dog ate it. If you have any doubt about the nature of temperamentally difficult children, please answer the following questions.

- If temperamentally difficult children, who don't care what their rooms look like, haven't been structured (consistently supervised until a habit is formed) to make their beds or to clean their rooms, is there any doubt what their rooms will look like?
- If temperamentally difficult children, who will walk through trash on the floor, haven't been structured to take out the trash on a regular schedule, is there any question what the kitchen floor will look like after one or two days?
- If temperamentally difficult children, who wouldn't notice or care if mildew filled the bathtub, aren't structured to leave the bathroom clean and orderly, is there any question what condition the bathroom will be left in?
- If temperamentally difficult children, who are bored by school, haven't been structured to study diligently and in an organized manner, is it likely that they will do well in high school or college?
- If temperamentally aggressive children, who enjoy controlling others, haven't been structured to stop bullying others, is it likely that they will stop on their own?
- If easily angered children are not structured to control their temper are they likely to treat their own children and spouses with patience and understanding?

If they aren't structured to do so, temperamentally difficult children will not control their anger or go out of their way to do anything that involves work or effort unless the task is also fun or exciting.

Because temperamentally difficult children are normally insensitive to the feelings of others, they have no idea why their parents and teachers get so upset, hurt, or angry when they do something wrong. Because they are so focused on "right now," they don't understand why parents get upset about what might have happened: "Hey, I put the fire out. The house didn't actually burn down. Why are you making such a big deal about a little gasoline in the kitchen?" Their misbehavior is impulsive and involves little forethought. As a result, punishment, rewards, and parents' lectures are of no use in changing their future behavior.

In general, if temperamentally difficult children feel like doing something, they do it. And if they don't feel like doing something— like classwork, homework, or chores—they either put it off as long as they can or, if confronted, use every excuse, lie, manipulation, and provocation they can muster, including temper tantrums, to get out of doing it. Anything that interferes with their doing what they want to do right now, frustrates and angers them, including confrontations about their misbehavior.

When punished for doing something wrong, most temperamentally difficult children become frustrated and angry, because they don't feel like being punished *now*. It makes no difference whether the punishment is grounding, spanking, extra work, or withdrawal of privileges. It doesn't matter whether the parents' consequences are logical or natural. It doesn't even matter if the children, as a part of an agreement or contract, previously chose and agreed to submit to their own punishment; they still don't feel like being punished *now*.

Instead of recognizing that their punishment is directly related to their misbehavior, they feel it as an unprovoked attack against them personally. And instead of learning that stopping the misbehavior stops the punishment, they typically dig in and endure any punishment as long as they can keep doing what they want to do. Temperamentally difficult children also rarely feel responsible for their wrongdoing and usually blame others for the trouble they cause.

Temperament in large part explains why some families have one black sheep among several well-behaved children. It also explains why so many adult criminals were abused as children. Many researchers have found that most habitual criminals were severely abused in childhood and blame abusive parents for creating criminals, but they ignore the fact that *temperamentally difficult children often provoke harsh punishment and abuse*. In fact, once they learn how to do so, many temperamentally difficult children control their parents by deliberately provoking them, sometimes for years on end.

Parents, of course, have their own set of temperamental traits which, when matched with their children's, can produce everything from relative peace and harmony to misery and anguish. Temperamentally difficult parents, determined to have their own way, who adopt or give birth to temperamentally difficult children, frequently find themselves in never-ending conflicts with their children. And passive parents with even one aggressive child, especially passive single parents with little or no emotional support, can be quickly worn down by an aggressive child's constant badgering. In fact, any combination of negative temperament traits shared between parents and children, unless controlled or changed, is likely to produce continuing frustration, anger, chaos, and depression.

Fortunately, by structuring new habit patterns, parents can learn to overcome their impulses, just as they want their children to do. When parents and other adults working with temperamentally difficult children build a positive structure, all but the most severely damaged children will respond well.

Temperamentally difficult children also use the aggressive controlling skills they have honed at home to control their neighbors, their teachers, and especially their peers. Many otherwise well-behaved children start to misbehave only after they have come under the powerful influence of temperamentally difficult children who have learned how to successfully control and exploit others to get their way.

Attention Deficit Disorder (ADD)

The temperament of young delinquents, gangsters, and criminals is almost identical to the characteristics used in diagnosing the presence of attention deficit disorder, a medical diagnosis applied to impulsive children and adults who have a difficult time staying focused on specific tasks, or attention deficit disorder with hyperactive syndrome, a medical diagnosis generally applied to impulsive children and adults who, in addition to having a difficult time staying focused on specific tasks, also tend to be highly aggressive. In fact, there is such a high correlation between the temperament of criminals and that of individuals who suffer from attention deficit disorder that many professionals believe that the leading cause of crime and violence is ADD.

There is a long-standing controversy over attention deficit disorder. Is it a true neurological disorder that impairs its victims' ability to control themselves, or is it nothing more than normal human behavior reflected on the high end of the continuum measuring human temperament and concentration? Although there are creditable experts on both sides of the question, no conclusive research proves the existence of attention deficit disorder. Further, no tests, machines, high-tech electronics, or computer programs can accurately diagnose it. Those children diagnosed by physicians as having ADD are assessed either through the subjective observation of their impulsive behavior or on behavior reported by parents, teachers, and others.

What is known is that most of the children diagnosed with ADD have a difficult time concentrating only on things that bore them. Unfortunately, many things bore them. Cleaning the kitchen bores them, of course. Yard work bores them. Learning to spell bores them, as does math. In fact, almost anything that is difficult, challenging, or in any way unpleasant bores them.

Interestingly, though, most of these children who can't concentrate on a household chore or homework for more than a few minutes can play computer games, listen to their favorite music, or watch television for hours at a time. Other, more sophisticated children diagnosed as suffering from ADD have no problem concentrating long enough to steal money from their parents and other family members or to set up a drug distribution system or to plan and execute a series of burglaries.

Over the past few years many books have been published on the problems associated with attention deficit disorder, some of them well researched and comprehensive, others less so. But after all has been thought out, debated, and discussed, the only issue that really matters regarding attention deficit disorder is whether to medicate or not medicate impulsive and aggressive children. Many impulsive and aggressive children who have a difficult time concentrating on schoolwork and household chores do calm down and concentrate better after being placed on pharmaceutical stimulants. But it is also true that almost all of the children diagnosed as having attention deficit disorder will also follow home and school rules without any drugs—when adult-imposed levels of discipline and supervision are increased enough to meet their individual needs. Unfortunately, for some highly aggressive and impulsive children that means almost one-on-one supervision until they develop and habituate the behavioral structures imposed by their parents, teachers, and in extreme cases, institutional house parents, counselors, or wilderness staff. Grandparents are omitted from this list because, although there are exceptions, most out-of-control children quickly wear out and grind down their grandparents. In other words, getting highly aggressive, impulsive children to behave takes a lot of time and effort—more time and effort than some mothers and fathers can provide. And if medication can temper a child's aggressiveness and bring it back within a parent's ability to control, it makes sense to use it. Although many parents are reluctant to force their children to take drugs of any kind, including those that are legally prescribed, helping restore the authority of emotionally overwhelmed parents should always be a top priority.

There are, however, reasons for not medicating children diagnosed as having ADD. These include the danger of side effects in some children—some serious enough to preclude the use of drug treatment—and the fact that many children with ADD symptoms don't respond to drug therapy. (Some even get worse with drug treatment.) And finally, some children refuse to cooperate and won't take their medication—because they don't like the way it makes them feel, because it makes them feel they are losing control, or because they are in a continuing power struggle with their parents and won't do anything their mothers or fathers want them to do. Don't worry, however, if you are in this situation. The recommendations set out elsewhere in this book will show you how to control even the most difficult children's behavior.

All in all, most out-of-control children don't need to be medicated, but if yours do, then do it, remembering that all children, including those diagnosed with ADD and ADDHS, need consistent discipline and supervision appropriate to their individual needs.

Structure, Ethological Milieus, and Bad Habits

Human behavior is formed, shaped, and for the most part controlled by the elements within the ethological milieus in which we live, work, and play. Those elements include the rules, beliefs, values, habits, and attitudes of the people with whom we spend our lives, especially those to whom we are emotionally attached. Children, like adults, tend to take on the characteristics of the ethological milieu in which they spend their time. If they spend most of their time with adults, they tend to take on the rules, beliefs, values, habits, and attitudes practiced and enforced by those adults. If those adults live in chaos, the children will live chaotic lives. If they live in an organized, disciplined environment, the children will tend to be organized and disciplined. And children who spend much of their time with other children tend to take on the rules, beliefs, values, habits, and attitudes of those children, for better or for worse.

Out-of-control children, even young criminals and gangsters, can be structured to behave well and to lead well-organized lives by enforcing the rules from their family's ethological milieu. Rules are enforced through the consistent application of discipline, supervision, and emotional attachment between children and parents. If family and community rules are consistently enforced, most out-of-control children can be brought back under control to lead productive, happy lives. By failing to consistently enforce rules, however, even otherwise easy-to-raise children can be permanently structured to live chaotic, disorganized lives. There is no issue, however, about whether children can be "trained" to behave. The only issue is who will provide the training: the children themselves, their peers, television, producers of music videos and movies, musical groups, or the adults that love them and care about them.

Structuring children to be organized, self-disciplined, and generally well behaved is a vital part of being a parent and should be an important goal of everyone who works with children, especially out-of-control children. Unless temperamentally difficult children are taught to control themselves they will continue to act on impulse and emotion, habituating impulsive behavior into lifelong problems, with a high likelihood of passing these habits, and the chaos they produce, on to their children. Even the most difficult

children, however, can be trained to be well behaved, well organized, and self-disciplined. They can be structured to be good husbands and wives, effective mothers and fathers, industrious
students, dependable workers, and considerate neighbors.

Few of us have been structured to behave well in all areas of our
lives. Most of us have habituated some types of behavior that serve
us well, some that serve us marginally, and some that truly serve us
badly. But the more structured our behavior is, and the greater the
number of well-structured rules and standards we follow, in general, the better we live our lives. The same is true for our children.

WHY CHILDREN'S BEHAVIOR NEEDS TO BE STRUCTURED

Children aren't born with a ready-made structure of "rights" and
"wrongs" to guide their behavior. And they certainly aren't born
with an acute desire always to please their parents. Unless structured otherwise, children and adults generally act on impulse and
emotion, doing what they please when they please. And if they
aren't structured with rules, values, beliefs, and behaviors that
create good character and good habits, their lives and the lives of
those around them will be chaotic.

Even easy-to-discipline children, whether they are seven or seventeen years old, won't, on their own initiative, clean up the dog's
mess, the yard, their rooms, or the kitchen they dirtied, without a
structure of rule-based discipline requiring them to do so. And if
they are temperamentally difficult children, the likelihood of them
using their own initiative to consistently do unpleasant or disagree-
able tasks like chores and schoolwork or treating their sister kindly,
is about as likely as the Congress of the United States giving itself a
pay cut.

A child's decision to misbehave almost always has an emotional
logic that is readily understandable. The following situations should
clarify for most parents why children, especially temperamentally
difficult children, frequently don't do what we want them to. Assume that none of the children in these examples have been structured to follow any particular rules in the situations presented.

*You are a temperamentally difficult eleven-year-old boy who has been
burdened with a "perfect" fourteen-year-old sister who never does anything wrong. As you sit at the kitchen table eating breakfast and watching*

cartoons, she gathers up dirty clothes without being told to do so and walks past you with a big armload of laundry. Her vision is partially blocked by the clothes in her arms. What are you likely to do?

- Get up and take some of the laundry out of her hands so she can see clearly.
- Show her she isn't as perfect as she thinks by tripping her and then telling her to watch where she's going.

You are a typical twelve-year-old girl who enjoys playing Nintendo, but your mother wants you to stop and clean your room. What are you likely to do?

- Pause your game, even though you are further than you have ever been in this game before.
- Ignore your mother and continue to play until you finish the game, or until your mother comes and gets you.

You are an impulsive fifteen-year-old boy in a garage with three of your friends and a slightly retarded thirteen-year-old girl. One of your friends has promised to give the girl a reward if she will take her clothes off and orally copulate all four of you. You are sexually excited watching your friends fondle the girl. What are you likely to do?

- Tell your friends that what they are doing is wrong, and take the girl home to her parents.
- Drop your pants.

You are a temperamentally difficult fourteen-year-old girl who wants to wear more makeup and less clothing than your unreasonable, mean mother allows — just as your friends do. You leave for school twenty minutes after your mother goes to work. What are you likely to do?

- Go to school dressed and made up just as your mother wants.
- Use your twenty unsupervised minutes to load up on makeup, change your clothes, and go to school looking like your friends.

You are an impulsive seventeen-year-old boy who was raised in a religious home to be tolerant and accepting of others, regardless of their race or ethnic background, but you enjoy the intense feeling of power and control that you feel when you wear your skinhead "uniform," especially when you are out in public with your racist fellow skinheads. One night while five of *you cruise around town looking for excitement, one of your buddies spots two young Central American immigrants walking down the street. Slamming on the brakes, the boy says, "Let's teach these assholes a lesson." What are you likely to do?*

- Tell your friends that what they plan to do is wrong and you won't have any part of it.
- Join the group, yelling, "Go back where you came from," while kicking and spitting on the two men.

Unless structured to behave otherwise, children, especially temperamentally difficult children, generally act on impulse and emotion.

The Results of Structuring

Fortunately, or unfortunately, depending on how well their children behave, parents don't have to wait until their children grow up to see the fruits of their labor. The difference between how well-structured children lead their daily lives in comparison to marginally or badly structured children is obvious.

Children who have been well structured get out of bed on their own, get ready for school without parents having to nag or yell, do their chores without a hassle, get to school on time, do their class assignments and homework, and come home when they are supposed to. Their attitudes toward adults are generally pleasant and cooperative. While they may spend a lot of time with their friends during the day, they are almost always in an adult-supervised environment at school, church, extracurricular activities, jobs, or home.

Most marginally structured kids eventually do what they are supposed to do, but usually only under duress. They get out of bed after several reminders. Getting them into and out of the bathroom in the morning is a major task. They frequently "forget" to clean their rooms or do their other chores. And it is astounding how many of their teachers don't assign homework, or how often their homework is lost, forgotten, or stolen. They also seem unable to tell time, as they are often late. Their attitude toward adults varies from pleasant to awful. They spend more time with their friends and peers than they do with adults.

Badly structured children either don't get out of bed or resist getting out of bed until their parents give up. They don't do chores, even when reminded. If they go to school at all, they are frequently late, or they leave early. And the idea of doing schoolwork of any kind is a joke to them. They come and go as they please, and they think that curfews are for other kids. Their attitude toward adults stinks. They rarely participate in family, church, or school activities, and while they may work part-time, they usually don't hold on to a job for very long. They spend several hours a day without direct or even indirect adult supervision, and parents generally don't know where these children are, who they are with, or what they are doing. Their conversation is generally profane and fixed on negative behavior; "And then I shoved my dick into her mouth so she'd blow me." "But she's only twelve years old, isn't she?" "Hey, if she's old enough to bleed, she's old enough to fuck."

3

BEHAVIORAL TEMPLATES

Behavioral templates are logical constructs used to understand and explain human habit patterns. Like all templates, they duplicate the patterns previously built on them. Human beings are creatures of habit. We habitualize our behavior patterns on templates that control most of our day-to-day behavior. Our eating is controlled by habit, in large part, dictating how, what, and when we eat; and it's virtually impossible for us to lose weight without substituting an entirely new eating and exercise pattern for the old one. What we drink, how we drink, and when we drink is also dictated by habit, and a recovering alcoholic who used to stop at a tavern with his friends after work, drink three or four beers, smoke several cigarettes, and play a couple of games of pool or shuffleboard, is going to be overwhelmed by the desire to drink a beer if he goes into that particular tavern, especially if he goes after work, meets his drinking buddies, lights up a cigarette, and plays a game of pool or shuffleboard.

New behavioral templates are created for each new habit. At birth the few templates that exist contain little more than the influences of one's inherited personality and temperament. But over the next several years, countless new templates are created to accommodate the structures that guide and define virtually all of our day-to-day behavior. And, whatever is built on those templates, good or bad, will be available to be repeated over and over for a lifetime, including character values, social skills, work patterns, organizational skills, driving styles, and sexual practices. Even how we talk to one another, the attitudes we share, the mannerisms we use, and how we argue are habituated.

It is not unusual for a mature, relatively well adjusted forty-five-year-old grandmother to walk into her sixty-five-year-old mother's home and find herself embroiled in an argument that has continued, off and on for thirty years. She and her mother sound the same, have the same attitudes, even use the same words from thirty years earlier. Forty-five-year-old Mom may even allow a fifteen-year-old's sigh of disgust to slip through her lips, just as she did thirty years earlier. Or she can walk into a room where her husband is on the telephone, and just by recognizing the attitude in his voice, be able to say, "Oh, say hi to your mom for me." These habits and behavior patterns are firmly built on the behavioral templates that all of us start using early in life.

In the home, children usually habituate the behavior built on their templates by their parents. When parents consistently monitor chores on a schedule, that schedule is built on their children's behavioral templates. If parents don't have a schedule for children's chores, children are structured to habitually wait for reminders. Parents who nag three or four times before following through to make sure that chores get done are teaching their children to procrastinate three or four times before doing their chores. And parents who follow through and make their children do chores only when they are angry are teaching their children to put off doing their chores until their parents get angry. Worse yet, the children learn to associate anger with obedience.

If we are consistently structured in childhood to be well-organized students or well-organized housekeepers of either sex, those organizational skills will be solidly built on our templates to be used whenever we do similar tasks in the future. If, on the other hand, our parents don't consistently monitor our household chores or our studies, and we can avoid doing them, those experiences will also be solidly built on our behavioral templates. And when we find ourselves in situations where we need good work habits or study skills, all we have to draw on is avoidance and procrastination. One of the reasons many husbands tend to do less housework and poorer-quality housework than their wives is that they continue to use the behavioral templates that were built in their childhood with the help of their parents. Finally, those parents who don't require children to do household tasks, or who give up in frustration and do the chores themselves, structure their children to do nothing, often for a lifetime. Interestingly, most of

America's delinquents and young criminals have no chores to do at home.

Emotional responses are also built on our behavioral templates, and they powerfully influence how we behave. If a child feels defeated in the first grade because her fine motor skills aren't as well developed as those of her peers, and no matter how hard she works her assignments are never as good as theirs, she may feel defeated whenever she has schoolwork to do in the future, even when she is fully capable of doing the work. A child with a strong aversion to reading because of a learning disability may hate to read long after he has learned how, because of the strong anti-reading feelings built on his behavioral template. And many inner-city black students, who are put down by their peers for "acting white" when they work hard and get good grades, build those negative feelings about working hard onto their templates to take with them to college or into the job market.

Even good feelings can present serious lifetime problems for children. An eight-year-old boy who over a two-year period is introduced to oral and anal sex by the eight- and ten-year-old boys down the street, and who enjoys having sex with little boys, will have those emotionally pleasurable experiences solidly built on a behavioral template—to battle or give in to for a lifetime. A seventeen-year-old who enjoys the camaraderie and experience of getting drunk or stoned at fraternity parties will repeatedly build those pleasurable feelings on a template—to feel and confront for a lifetime—and the younger he is when he starts using drugs or alcohol, the stronger the habit will be.

Some parents may not want the responsibility of providing the foundation templates for their children's ultimate success or failure in life, but there is no way to avoid it. Even the chaotic results of doing nothing are permanently built on children's templates. The question, then, is what should or should not be built on them? Parents can purposefully build their children's templates for a high likelihood of success, a moderate likelihood of success, or complete life failure. Children's templates can be built to include good study skills, disorganized and ineffective study skills, no study skills, or a hatred for studying. They can be built with productive work habits, poor work habits, or a strong aversion to work. They can be structured for self-sufficiency or lifelong dependency, for honesty and integrity or for criminality, for sobriety or for drug and alcohol dependency, for honor or for dishonor.

Temperamentally difficult children, already at high risk from birth for most of life's worst situations, tend to aggravate their problems even more by habituating their impulsive, disruptive behavior patterns. Arguing, lying, throwing tantrums, making threats, or using physical intimidation and violence are frequently structured onto difficult children's templates, where they will serve to control, disrupt, and overwhelm the lives of others, often for a lifetime.

On the other hand, the behavioral templates of temperamentally difficult children can be structured by adults to reduce the impulsiveness that creates many of their problems. They can be structured to control their temper and stop hitting or hurting others. Even those temperamentally difficult boys who would otherwise grow up to beat the women and children in their homes can be trained to control their temper and their violent behavior. Other difficult children can be structured away from crime, drug and alcohol abuse, teenage sex and pregnancy, and all other behavior patterns associated with impulsiveness—before these problems are given a chance to get started. But even if children do get off to a bad start and become involved in crime, gangs, drugs, and dropping out, most parents, given enough time, can help them build new structures to override those that are out of date, flawed, self-defeating, or criminal. Only those adults whose template bases were irreparably damaged in childhood by chronic neglect, severe abuse, or abandonment are possibly beyond being helped.

Structuring Templates for Success or Failure

Children's behavioral templates can be structured with good character traits, good habits, and positive attitudes by using the three elements within the ethological milieu that structure children's behavior: *rule-based discipline, supervision, and emotional attachment.* These three elements are irreplaceable if difficult children and delinquent young adults are to ever lead worthy lives. No substitutions can be made. Nothing can compensate for their loss. Nothing.

And the longer they are missing, the greater the likelihood that children's character, habit patterns, and attitudes will be permanently malformed, dysfunctional, and chaotic.

DISCIPLINE

Discipline consists of three elements: clearly defined and stated rules; follow-through and monitoring to make the rules mandatory; and consistency.

Clearly Defined and Stated Rules: Rules define and identify the specific composition of the structures built on children's templates.

To be effective rules must specify what to do, how to do it, when to do it, and how often to do it. Or, with negative behavior such as stealing and drug use, the rule must specify what not to do and how long to follow the rule. Even if parents are sure that their children completely understand the rules and responsibilities of their homes, they should continue to specify what the children are to do (or not do) until they dependably do it right. Otherwise, many children will continue to do things their way rather than follow the rules.

Follow-Through and Monitoring to Make the Rules Mandatory: Follow-through and monitoring help children understand that they have to follow the rules as set out, that there is no choice.

To ensure that they obey and habituate family and school rules, children need adult monitoring based on the level of trust they earn and the level of responsibility they assume. Children who accept a great deal of responsibility and earn a maximum amount of trust in a specific situation will need a minimum of adult monitoring and follow-through. Children who accept no responsibility and earn no trust in any specific situation will need a maximum amount of adult monitoring and follow-through. For instance, a sixteen-year-old girl who is good about getting out of bed in the morning but awful about picking up the mess she makes in her room and in the bathroom needs a minimum amount of parental monitoring and follow-through to get out of bed, but a high level of direct monitoring and follow-through when she is to clean her room and the bathroom. In another typical example, a thirteen-year-old boy who is completely dependable about feeding and watering his dog, moderately dependable about taking out the trash, and completely undependable about taking care of the yard need a minimal amount of parental monitoring and follow-through when he is to take care of the dog, a moderate amount of monitoring and follow-through when it's time to take out the trash, and a maximum level of monitoring and follow-through when it's time to take care of the yard.

As children accept more responsibility and earn more trust, the level of adult monitoring and follow-through will drop accordingly. But children who are even temporarily irresponsible automatically lose trust and earn a higher level of adult monitoring and follow-through.

Consistency versus Inconsistency: Consistency gives strength and longevity to the structure built on children's behavioral templates. Inconsistency weakens and damages everything it touches, producing gaps, rips, holes, and chaos in the structures parents build for their children.

If parents consistently enforce rules based on earned trust levels, children will consistently obey those rules. If parents inconsistently enforce their rules, children will obey inconsistently, at best. The more inconsistently parents enforce their rules, the more vigorously children will fight them, and the more they fight, the angrier they and their parents will become. In fact, the primary reason for parent-child anger in most homes is inconsistently enforced rules. If parents, for example, consistently monitor their children's whereabouts and follow through, as necessary, to make sure that they are in the house every school night at six o'clock to do their homework, children will virtually never fight coming in, because they expect to come in at six o'clock. If, however, parents inconsistently monitor their children's whereabouts, so that the kids learn that they can sometimes stay out until six-ten, six-thirty, seven o'clock, or later, they will constantly fight coming in, not only on those nights when parents try to get them in at six o'clock, but virtually every other night as well. Their experience has demonstrated that sometimes they can stay out later, so that is what they expect to be able to do.

Paradoxically, when parents are often inconsistent, children are conditioned to challenge authority, break rules, and disrupt their classrooms and neighborhoods, as well as to fight anyone who tries to stop them. It's better for everyone, parents and children included, to have no rules than to have rules that are inconsistently enforced.

Some parents are periodically inconsistent, treating children's discipline and supervision like a diet. They do the work necessary to get their children's behavior under control. But once things are in place, they abandon the plan. And just as fat inevitably returns to the wayward dieter's body, children will revert to old behavior patterns and attitudes when parents stop monitoring and supervising their behavior. Even well-behaved, responsible young people need to know that Mom or Dad will be checking up on them periodically.

Inconsistency is just as damaging to relationships as it is to behavioral structures. Inconsistently given love and caring will eventually destroy even a well-meaning family. No relationship, even if it started with close parent-child attachment, can sustain itself if love and caring aren't faithfully and dependably there to nurture it.

SUPERVISION

Supervision means consistently knowing and approving of what your children are doing, where they are, and, most important, who they are with.

By knowing and approving of where your children are, you can help them to stay away from potentially dangerous and corrupting ethological milieus. Along with physically dangerous places, children, especially temperamentally difficult children, should not be in socially dangerous places where they are given the freedom to break family and school rules and are often encouraged to do so.

By knowing and approving of what your children are doing, you can keep them away from harmful activities. Unless parents openly condone it, children can abuse drugs and alcohol, join gangs, commit crimes, vandalize property, or have sex only if their parents don't know what they are doing. Someone at this point usually says, "But I can't watch them twenty-four hours a day." The good news is that parents can provide their children with excellent supervision twenty-four hours a day, without having to do all of it themselves.

By knowing and approving of the people your children are with, you can keep temperamentally difficult children away from negative peers.

If your children become emotionally attached to even one negative friend or to a corrupt peer culture, there is a high probability they will start to mimic the values, attitudes, and actions of that friend or group, eventually building conforming behavioral structures on their own behavioral templates. Overcoming the powerful influence of negative peers takes considerable time and energy, but it is one of the most important things parents can do to protect their children.

As I have said, parents need to know and approve of where their children are, what they are doing, and who they are with. But of all the concerns parents need to address in supervising their children, the most important one by far is making sure they don't come under the influence of negative peers and associates.

It is vital for your children's well-being that you monitor and oversee their peer associations and friendships. Meet all of your children's friends and their parents. And use the following classification system to determine which kids your children may associate with and the level of supervision each one needs.

A-category kids are the ones you know well. Their parents share and enforce the same basic rules that you do, and they supervise their children well. These children do well in school, respect adult authority at home and at school, participate in school, community, or church activities, may have part-time employment, and follow the rules their parents and teachers set out. A-category children are trustworthy, responsible, and caring.

A-category children can have a lot of freedom. Depending on their age, they can go to movies, basketball games, shopping, school activities, skating, and bowling without direct adult supervision. But even A-category kids shouldn't go to teenage nightclubs, parties, or rock concerts without immediate and direct adult supervision, if even then.

B-category kids are ones you don't know well yet or whose parents you don't know yet. They may also be kids whom you know very well, but they certainly aren't A-category kids, and to the best of your knowledge they aren't C-category kids. Or they are kids who seem solid and straight but whose parents are unreliable and irresponsible and don't provide an adequate level of supervision. Generally B-category kids aren't yet fully trustworthy and responsible. Children you have just met and haven't yet categorized should be given a temporary B rating until you get to know them better. B-category kids can go almost everywhere that A-category kids can go, but they need responsible adults to go with them.

C-category kids are untrustworthy or irresponsible. Any child who uses drugs, tobacco, or alcohol is automatically a C-category kid. So are kids who are in gangs or other negative peer cultures, kids who steal or commit other crimes, kids who run away or cut school, and kids who lie to you. C-category kids should have no contact with your children at all, in person, on the telephone, or via letters and notes.

Please keep in mind that children can change categories. An A-category kid can drop to the C category with the first puff of marijuana, the first swig of vodka, the first shoplifting episode, or the first lie to you about your child. Children can also move up, but it takes a long time to rebuild trust that has been betrayed, and the move from C to B may take months.

Methods of Enforcement: If you can't trust your children to stay away from their B- or C-category friends, don't let them go out of the house unless you or another responsible adult can go with them. If you can't turn your back without your children sneaking out of the house to be with their friends, secure your home. Install double-key dead-bolt locks on the front and back doors. Secure sliding glass doors and children's bedroom windows with locks or other appropriate devices. Or, for kids who are less aggressive and challenging, install relatively inexpensive alarms that will alert you the instant the children try to sneak out of their rooms.

If you need to secure your home to protect your children, it is vital that you install or check smoke detectors, and design and practice emergency escape plans in case of fire. Never lock a child in a room. Instead, secure the window and place an alarm on the door—Radio Shack sells them for less than $10—or a motion-sensor alarm in the hallway. Never lock a child of any age in a house or apartment and then leave. Never lock a child out of the house overnight or after school. If the child is so untrustworthy that you need to consider a lockout, then he or she clearly needs a high level of supervision.

Now, before you get excited and upset because of what you may have to do to regain control of an out-of-control child, look at it this way. If your two-year-old son learned to open up the front door and run out to the street, you would put a lock of some sort on that door that day. But the two-year-old would be safer out on the street— because someone would be likely to pick him up and attempt to find out where he lived—than your out-of-control seventeen-year-old son. Every child needs to be supervised based on the level of trust he or she has earned. And a seventeen-year-old boy who sneaks out of his bedroom window or runs out the front door to snort dope, get drunk, steal, or hang out with gangsters has earned the same level of trust and supervision as the two-year-old who also runs out of the house to get his way.

One of the best ways to keep kids out of trouble is to keep them busy and occupied with constructive, worthwhile, and fun activities. The busier children are, the harder it is for them to get into trouble. Do your best to encourage their talents and interests. If your daughter or son has a natural talent or special interest in music, dance, athletics, drawing, writing, building, helping, acting, studying, composing, painting, or exploring, push the child toward that activity. Enroll your children in classes, or help them find jobs or volunteer work where they will be needed. (Helping the very young or the very old is especially rewarding for most teenagers.) One of the benefits of keeping children busy with organized activities is that they spend most of their time with responsible adults and well-structured children who can help pull them up and away from friends who are a bad influence.

Making sure that difficult children are involved in enjoyable and worthwhile activities should never be considered a reward for good behavior—a reward that can be removed if the child behaves badly. These activities form part of the foundation for habituating good behavior. With adequate adult monitoring and supervision they provide the opportunity for building solid, well-built behavior patterns onto children's behavioral templates for a lifetime of good use.

EMOTIONAL ATTACHMENT

Attachment, or bonding, includes time together, dependability, and emotional and physical affection. Parents who aren't attached to their children tend to be unwilling to do the hard and necessary work to adequately discipline and supervise their children. Tragically, some temperamentally difficult children are difficult to attach to from birth. Others, especially teenagers with negative peers, become emotionally detached from loving parents as they bond with their friends.

Children who aren't bonded with their parents tend to make little effort to please their parents' or to conform to their expectations.

Until they can be rebonded—and most can be—they are the kids who are most likely to be violent, drop out of school, abuse drugs and alcohol, make babies early, commit serious crimes, and live on the streets.

In general, the more time parents and children spend together without anger, especially in activities that are fun and enjoyable, the greater the level of attachment. But even time spent doing homework or household chores can bring children and parents closer together. Every time parents sit through two hours of a school talent show just to see their child dance or sing for five minutes, they reinforce their special relationship. The same is true of parents who watch their children play sports or act in a play or who go to a school open house to talk to their children's teachers. And it's also true when children regularly participate in religious programs with their parents.

Children must be able to count on their parents physically and emotionally being there for them, as needed. When they can't, children either start to withdraw into themselves emotionally or misbehave.

Affection and caring words—hugs, kisses, scratched backs, rubbed shoulders, and expressions of love, caring, appreciation, and thanks—are also important elements in creating a bond between adults and children.

Structural Flaws

Most persistent childhood misbehavior, as well as the chaos it produces, results from structural flaws permanently embedded in children's behavioral templates. These flaws are created when one or more of the elements of rule-based discipline are missing or incomplete: when rules have not been adequately defined or the level of adult monitoring and follow-through has not met the child's needs, or when there has been a lack of consistency in enforcing the rules. Structural flaws are also created by a lack of adequate supervision, when parents don't know and approve of where children are, who they are with, and what they are doing. Finally, when the parent-child bond is severely damaged or missing, structural flaws are inevitable.

Unflawed structuring requires that the rules forming children's behavioral structure be mandatory and that they always be obeyed—with occasional exceptions for good cause, of course. When children are young, parents enforce mandatory rules without giving it a second thought. In most homes, if a five-year-old boy wants to watch television rather than take a bath, he has to take a bath. Even if he throws a tantrum or argues and yells, Mom or Dad at some point will make him take a bath. They may have to carry him to the bathtub. They may have to help him scrub his body. They may have to dry him off. But he will take a bath. And if parents are consistent he will structure scheduled bathing onto his behavioral template.

While proximity and close monitoring are usually all that is needed to get an older child to complete a task or follow a rule, there are times when parents may have to "help" uncooperative children get out of bed by pulling the covers off their bodies and physically removing them from the bed. Or parents may occasionally need to take their truant children to school and walk them from class to class. If they are consistent, however, children will quickly begin following these mandatory rules on their own.

Judges understand and use the concept of mandatory rules better than anyone. If a juvenile court judge has directed people, including witnesses, to appear in court and they don't show up, the judge will direct the bailiff to find the people and bring them to court, by force if necessary. If juvenile defendants won't stay seated in court, the judge will eventually order the bailiff to tie them to a chair or to remove them from the courtroom. If after repeated admonishments defendants won't keep quiet, the judge will have them gagged or removed from the courtroom. If they won't leave on their own, the judge will order the bailiff to remove them. If they violently resist, they will be subdued, restrained, shackled, and carried to a holding room. Keep in mind, however, that force is used *only if the people involved make it necessary.*

In one way or another, the rules governing behavior in court will be enforced and obeyed. No choice is allowed. When it becomes obvious that a juvenile defendant, who has nothing to lose if held in contempt of court, isn't going to cooperate and follow the rules of the court, the judge won't argue, reason, lecture, or resort to punishment. He or she will simply require that the bailiff "help" the child to behave as directed. Fortunately, that level of force is rarely needed in court because judges typically monitor and consistently follow through to enforce their orders and because virtually all defendants know they don't really have a choice. The same can be true at home and school. When difficult children understand that they truly don't have a choice and when parents and teachers monitor and follow through at a child's demonstrated level of trust, kids will obey and follow the rules set out by their parents and teachers.

However, if parents typically tell their children two or three times to take a bath, clean their room, or do homework before following through and monitoring to see that it is done promptly, the children will correctly assume from their experience that the rules aren't mandatory and that they don't have to obey their parents all the time. The same is true when children repeatedly badger parents until they give up and give in, and when parents rely on punishments, rewards, natural consequences, counseling, or the "school of hard knocks" to get children to behave—because all of these methods offer children a choice when it comes to behaving. The same is true of schools that don't effectively monitor their campuses to keep students in class but instead punish those truants who are caught. This is especially true of schools that suspend students for truancy: "Sir, do I have this right? Because I was truant on Monday and Tuesday, you aren't going to let me come to school on Thursday and Friday? Ah, that's rough. I've sure learned my lesson." It is also true of teachers who don't check homework and in-class assignments. If, when assignments are due, teachers say nothing about those not turned in, it is obvious to the students that completing the assignments and turning them in isn't mandatory. And if rules aren't mandatory they don't have to be obeyed. Perhaps they are supposed to be obeyed, or they should be obeyed, perhaps others would like them to be obeyed, and perhaps someone will be punished if they aren't obeyed, but if they aren't enforced as mandatory rules, they don't have to be consistently obeyed.

Flawed Discipline: Inconsistency and Chaos

Inconsistency destroys virtually everything it touches. Inconsistently enforced rules result in anger, resentment, frustration, rage, and chaos for everyone involved. Inconsistently given love—love that is never dependably there—produces children who don't trust or bond with others and who are at risk for all of life's failures. And inconsistency is the single best way to train children to misbehave. Unfortunately, inconsistency is easy. As you will see below, unspecific and unclarified rules produce inconsistency. So do most of the unsuccessful methods parents use to change misbehavior.

NAGGING INCONSISTENCY

Mom, carrying four heavy bags of groceries, walked into the kitchen and saw a mess. Dirty dishes were scattered all over, the trash can was overflowing, the floor was covered with crumbs and something sticky. Setting the grocery bags on the floor, she yelled, "Scott, get in here and help me."

Hearing no response, she yelled again, "Scott, are you deaf? Get in here and help me."

"Yeah, I heard you," said fourteen-year-old Scott from the front room, where he was watching MTV.

Hearing his response, Mom started putting the groceries away. But after a few minutes she stopped and called again. "Damn it, Scott, I need help in here."

"Okay," Scott yelled impatiently, "I'll be right there." But he made it no further than the edge of the couch as a new video caught his attention.

Thinking he was on his way, Mom finished putting the groceries away, but realized her error when she tried to get the empty grocery sacks into the overflowing trash. "Scott," she screamed, as she marched into the front room, stopped, turned, and pointed back into the kitchen. "Turn off the TV right now and get into the kitchen."

"You don't have to yell," he screamed. "I was coming."

"Sure you were, after I put away all the groceries. Now, get in there and clean up the mess you made."

The only consistency in this family is that the same scene, or one very much like it, is played out between Mom and Scott virtually every evening. No firm rules have been set about dirtying or cleaning the kitchen, taking out the trash, or responding to Mom when she calls. And Mom didn't monitor and follow through to get Scott into the kitchen until after the fourth time she called him. Every time she called and he didn't come, she grew angrier. And each time she nagged, yelled, and interrupted his program, he grew angrier.

By the time Mom came to get him, neither one of them was fit to be around.

The Solution: Be consistent. Follow a schedule. Never stop monitoring, and never walk away from less than responsible children unless they are doing as you directed. Every time parents walk away before children are fully involved in completing their designated tasks, they structure them always to ignore Mom or Dad at least one more time.

RESCUERS AND INCONSISTENCY

They were at it again. As soon as she heard the fight, Mom ran to the family room, where Dad and thirteen-year-old Crystal were arguing. "Both of you be quiet," she yelled. They both shut up and looked at her. Crystal's eyes were encrusted with heavy dark makeup. Her lipstick was a bright red.

Mom walked past Dad, still sitting in his favorite chair, marched Crystal into the kitchen, and asked, "Now, what was going on in there?"

"Dad was ragging on me about my makeup, again."

"If you hadn't gone in there and provoked him he never would have said a thing."

"I was already watching television when he came in and started yelling at me, telling me I looked cheap and sleazy."

"You know how he is since he's been sick," she said impatiently. "Just stay away from him."

"Fuck him, I live here, too. Why do I have to stay away from him? He's the one with a problem."

"Let it be, damn it. I don't want you setting him off and giving him another heart attack."

Mom has made it clear that her husband's health problems are far more important than any rule about excessive makeup. Crystal knows Mom won't follow through and enforce the makeup rule because Dad might get upset, and she knows Dad won't enforce the rule because Mom won't let him. Crystal figures that she can do whatever she wants. The longer Mom acts as rescuer, the less consistently household rules will be enforced and the more Crystal will use confrontation to get her way. If this situation lasts long enough—several weeks will do—Crystal can be structured to be confrontational for a lifetime.

The Solution: Mom should stay focused on the rule or task at hand. Dad is not the real issue. Read about "Arguing," to learn what Mom needs to do to stay focused.

PARENTAL CONFLICT AND INCONSISTENCY

Fifteen-year-old Buddy was lying on his bed, propped up by pillows, listening to a CD through a set of headphones when Dad walked in. "I need to talk to you, kid," said Dad, tapping Buddy's headset.

"What?" snapped Buddy.

"We have to talk about you and Mom."

"She's not my mother."

"Okay," said Dad as he knelt beside Buddy. "We have to talk about you and your stepmother."

"I haven't done anything wrong. You and I got along fine until you married her."

"That's my fault. I let you slide on too many things. All she is trying to do is get us to keep the house picked up, including your bathroom and bedroom."

"She doesn't have to use my bathroom or even look into my bedroom. If she'd just leave me alone we'd get along fine."

"Well, that's not going to happen. She's not going to change. And please keep in mind that I have to live with her, too. I know her even better than you do."

"But you work a lot and aren't home as much as I am. You don't have to put up with it."

"You're wrong. I have to listen to it when I get home. So I'm asking you to do me a favor and quit fighting with her. Don't argue. Please go along with her until she calms down, okay."

It is impossible to be consistent if parents don't work together. Even though Buddy's dad sounds as if he somewhat supports Mom in getting Buddy to clean up after himself, he makes it clear that cleaning up is his wife's value, not his. Unless Dad changes his attitude and truly supports Mom, Buddy will continue to believe that he doesn't have to obey his stepmother. Whenever parents, stepparents, guardians, or parenting-again grandparents disagree about basic values and rules and fail to work together, inconsistency and its relatives—anger, frustration, and resentment—will appear.

The Solution: If you and your spouse agree to compromise or to follow the sample rules set out in this book, you will find yourselves and your children working well together. Another workable alternative for conflicting parents is to follow a single-parent strategy and designate one spouse to do all of the parenting while the other backs away and doesn't interfere. This approach isn't as good as two parents working together as a team, supporting one another and giving each other periods of rest, as needed. The single-parent approach can put a heavy strain on the marriage relationship, but it can work adequately.

If you and your spouse still can't agree to work together on the important issues related to children's discipline, supervision, and attachment, you are prime candidates for marriage counseling. Seek it out. If one or both of you refuse, it's a strong indicator of serious marriage problems unrelated to the children.

JOINT CUSTODY CONFLICTS AND INCONSISTENCY

Dawn opened the door, tossed her book bag on the backseat, and sat down next to her dad, who had custody of her during the coming week.

"How are you doing?" asked Dad.

"Okay," she said, discouraged.

"What's wrong?" he asked, pulling into traffic.

"It's Mom, of course."

"Now what's wrong?"

"Mom is being a bitch. She's never satisfied with what I do, and now she says I can't see Alex until my grades come up."

"I thought we had settled the Alex question," he said. "Are your grades bad?"

"No. I'm passing all my courses, including geometry. Mom is still trying to keep me away from Alex by inventing problems that don't exist.

"Well, don't worry about it when you're with me, although I don't approve of Alex either."

"Yeah, I know."

A week later Mom noticed that Dawn was sullenly looking out the windshield as she drove home. Even though experience had taught her to say nothing when Dawn was in one of her moods, Mom tried to reach out to her.

"Is something bothering you?"

"No," Dawn said curtly, not bothering to look at her mother.

"It's not good to keep things bottled up inside you."

"It won't make any difference if I do talk."

"Let's see."

"I don't see why I can't see Alex. Dad lets me."

"You are preoccupied with Alex. You got failure notices in three classes and D's in the others because you spend all of your time with Alex. Not to mention that he's a dropout and a drug user who's on probation and who slaps you around."

"I made up all my work. I'm not failing anything now," Dawn shouted.

"Don't yell at me," Mom said.

"Dad doesn't think I need to stay away from Alex. He thinks you push me too hard and that if you'd back off I'd do a lot better."

"I'm sure he does."

"You can't stop me from being with Alex."

"Don't tell me what I can't do."

"I'm not going to stop seeing him. I'll call Dad. He'll tell you."

As soon as they pulled into the driveway, Dawn ran into the house. By the time Mom walked in, she was on the phone.

"She won't even let me talk to him on the phone. . . . Well, will you tell her that? . . . Okay. . . . Dad wants to talk to you," she said and handed the telephone to Mom.

"Why do you want to talk to me?" Mom said when she took the phone. *"You said you wanted all of our issues handled by letter. . . . No, I understand you won't allow me to keep her away from Alex, but I can't believe you want her to fail this semester, too. . . . She's failing or almost failing everything. I sent the reports to you early last week. . . . Gee, that's a hard one. Who was living with you last week who had access to your mail? . . . Call the school, then. Do something novel. . . . Yes, she lies, even to her wonderful father. . . . Fuck you, too. . . . Okay, it's clear that you're never going to change and that I'm powerless to control Dawn, so you take her full time. I'll drive her over to your place tonight. . . . Inconvenient! You asshole,"* she screamed and slammed down the phone, overwhelmed with frustration and rage. *"Oh, no, I'm not going to keep playing this game,"* she said, and temporarily escaped from the house.

Dawn watched her mother leave and yelled out the front door for the neighborhood to hear, *"You always walk away. You won't even listen to Dad. . . . Fucking bitch."*

Consistency is almost impossible in joint custody arrangements. King Solomon only threatened to cleave a child in two to settle a custody dispute, but American judges do it all the time, with predictable results. If American divorce courts had purposefully set out to destroy the lives of as many children as they could, they couldn't have come up with a better device than joint physical custody where parents split the child's time and presence between them and jointly make most of the decisions affecting the child. It would be less abusive to many children to hit them in the head with a two-by-four than to subject them to the results of joint custody. Parents who couldn't work together when married are subsequently supposed to cooperate in raising their children— something that is difficult in the best of circumstances. Although some divorced parents manage to make joint custody arrangements work, the parents of temperamentally difficult children almost never do. More often than not such children keenly exploit the conflicts and resentments of their divorced or separated parents to get their way, producing chaos for everyone involved.

Because consistency is one of the most important elements in child development, the best approach is to give custody to the parent who historically and consistently has been the primary caregiver. The parent who, in general, bought the children's clothing, fixed their meals, took them to the doctor and dentist, made sure they were clean, took them to their dance classes, basketball practices and games, should have the right to continue that role without interference after a divorce. The other parent should have reasonable visitation rights.

Most cooperative divorced couples, including those with joint custody decrees, eventually settle into custody and visitation arrangements that somewhat meet their individual needs or the needs of their children, regardless of what the divorce court initially required them to do. But parents trapped in joint custody arrangements with spiteful, angry, controlling former spouses often spend years in emotional conflict and throw away thousands of dollars in attorneys' fees while their children continue to be destroyed.

The Solution: Divorce frequently hurts children. Don't compound a bad situation. Do everything possible to avoid joint physical custody. Let your attorney, the court conciliator, court-ordered therapists, and the judge know that even though they may not care about your child's well-being, you do. In fact, in many cases it is better to let your former spouse have custody and act as the primary caregiver than to subject the children to the misery of joint physical custody. The primary caregiver system gives primary caregivers the opportunity to raise their children with a maximum of consistency and a minimum of destructive interference from uncooperative former spouses. And the primary care-giver system is the only hope for many, if not all, temperamentally difficult children in divorce situations.

CHAOTIC INCONSISTENCY

The kitchen was a mess. Unwashed dishes caked with dried food overflowed the sink and mixed with the trash and garbage cluttering every counter. There was more trash on the floor than there was in the trash can and it formed an irregular path into the living room of the small apartment where Candy, eleven years old, and John, age eight, were watching Saturday morning television.

Dad's newest girlfriend, twenty-seven-year-old Lisa, dressed in white cotton panties and an oversized white T-shirt, shuffled through the front room to the kitchen in search of something to make her feel better. She looked in the cupboards and rooted through the litter on the counter in search of an aspirin or anything that would help clear her head.

"Candy, this place is a fuckin' mess," she yelled sluggishly. "Where in the hell is the aspirin?"

"Huh?" Candy asked, paying more attention to the television than to Lisa.

"Are you deaf? Where are the fuckin' aspirin?"

"Look in the bathroom."

"Shit!" yelled Lisa as she jammed her foot down on something sharp and unseen in the litter on the floor. "Damn, but that hurts." She reached down to rub the bottom of her foot. "Candy, get in here and clean this mess up."

"It's not my job," the girl said, still watching television. "John is supposed to take out the trash."

"So where's John?" asked Lisa as she limped into the front room.

"Don't know. He left a couple hours ago."

"Well, you clean it up, then."

"No. It's not my job, and you're not my mother."

"Don't you tell me no," Lisa said, looking Candy straight in the eye and yelling for her father. "Art, get in here and teach your daughter some manners."

"It's not my job," screamed Candy, sobbing. "John never does anything around here, and I have to do everything. It's not fair."

"What's going on now?" asked Dad, standing in the doorway in his underpants.

Still sobbing, Candy said, "She wants me to do John's job."

"This house is a fuckin' mess," said Lisa. "You never make these kids do anything. I asked Candy to clean up the trash after I jammed my foot into that mess on the kitchen floor."

Dad said to Candy, "Get in there and clean up the trash, like Lisa told you to, and don't give me any crap or back talk."

"But it's not my job," she screamed. "Go get John and make him do it.

Dad stepped over to Candy and slapped her face, hard. "Don't talk back to me, ever. If you're told to do something, just do it."

"But it's not my job," she sobbed, hunkering down into the couch.

"Goddammit, don't talk back to me! Now, get in the kitchen," he screamed, raising his hand to hit her again.

Candy threw herself to the floor and quickly crawled to the kitchen on her hands and knees. She picked up the full trash can and took it out to the trash bin. She didn't pick up any of the trash from the floor or the counters, nor did she wash any dishes. Neither Lisa nor Dad said anything to Candy or John about the continuing mess in the kitchen until two days later when Dad lost his temper while searching through the kitchen mess for his misplaced car keys.

Dad and his live-in girlfriend have no rules, no schedules, no job descriptions for taking out the trash, for cleaning dishes, floors, kitchen counters, sinks, or for doing any other household chore. It is unlikely that they have rules, schedules, or job descriptions about anything, including schoolwork and studying. Whatever the children are expected to do depends on the immediate impulse and whim of Dad and his girlfriend. The longer these children live in this environment of structured chaos, the more that chaos will be permanently stamped on their behavioral templates for a lifetime of misuse and will eventually be inflicted on yet another generation.

People raised in chaotic homes are at highest risk for complete life failure: dropping out of school, drug abuse, alcoholism, criminality, chronic unemployment, chronic and total unreliability, mental illness, homelessness, and the loss of their own children. And the greater the degree and longevity of the chaos, the greater the likelihood of life failure. Children raised in chaos or with a great deal of inconsistency are easily recognized. They are constantly angry and are likely to challenge rules, values, restrictions, and any other elements of structure placed in their way.

The Solution: Put yourself and the children on a consistent schedule and follow through and enforce your rules when the job is to be done, not after the fact. Always stay focused on the rule or task at hand rather than on your momentary feelings. Never focus on a person as the problem. Restructure the children's behavior through discipline, supervision, and attachment. If the conditions in your home are truly chaotic, you probably need the help of a counselor or parent-trainer to keep you on task while you build new behavioral templates to replace your old ones.

4
RULES

Missing or Poorly Defined Rules

When parents don't set and clearly define rules for their children, there are no rules to follow. And if there are no rules, children, especially difficult children, will do as they please, regardless of what adults would like them to do.

Unfortunately, parents of misbehaving children frequently fail to clearly define their rules. Perhaps they have tried, but many normal children, and all difficult children, do whatever they must to get their way, including using parents' words to their advantage. Most children actually know how their parents want them to behave, but they tend to be very literal in interpreting their parents' words, a practice known as minimal literalism—How little can I do and still be able to say "I did what you told me to do"?

THE NEED FOR A JOB DESCRIPTION

Fifteen-year-old Gary hung up the kitchen phone and called to his mother. "Mom, can I go to David's?"

Sylvia, on her hands and knees washing the bathroom floor, paused in her work and asked, "Have you watered the roses yet?"

"No."

"Then go do it. After the roses are watered, you can go to David's for a while."

"Shit," Gary said under his breath. He went into the garage, threw the hose down by the nearest rosebush, connected it to the spigot, and turned the water on as hard as it would go. A hard stream blasted a hole in the well

around the first plant, washed away most of the dirt around the roots of the second bush, and overflowed into the well holding the third rosebush before cascading down the street. Deciding his work was sufficiently done, Gary left the water running and hurried to David's.

Twenty minutes later he was shocked to find his mother at David's front door. "What's wrong, Mom?"

"You were supposed to water the roses before you went to David's."

"I did."

"You got water on three plants and left it on to run down the street."

"You're never satisfied. I did what you told me to do. You didn't say I had to water all of them before I left. I was going to get the rest when I got back home. Nobody's perfect, you know."

Primary Problem: Gary received no specific job description for watering the roses. Mom didn't tell him how many roses to water (all fifteen), how to water them (with a slow water flow), how much water each plant was to get (fill every well to the top), or what he was to do after he finished (turn the water off, rewind the hose, put it back in the garage, and then come and get his mother so that she could check the quality of his work).

The Need for a Job Description, a Schedule, and Direction

All morning long Christa nagged at Bart, her twelve-year-old son, to take out the kitchen trash. She nicely reminded him of the trash at 8:00 A.M. when he turned on the television ("Don't forget the trash, honey"). She reminded him again a little after 9:00 A.M. as she was carrying his dirty clothes through the front room ("The trash is still waiting"), again at 10:30 as she vacuumed the front room ("When are you going to get the trash?"), and once more at noon when she called him to lunch ("Just how long do you plan on leaving the trash overflowing onto the floor?") Her voice and temper became louder and sharper every time she reminded him of the trash.

After lunch, with Bart's dishes still sitting on the kitchen table and the overflowing trash littering the floor, Christa heard the television come back on in the front room and became the mother she had promised herself she would never be. "Get off your butt and take out the trash right now," she screamed as she turned off the television and chased Bart into the kitchen. "Every Saturday it's the same thing. I do all of the work around here and you watch television. I wash your clothes and you watch television. I scrub your toilet and you watch television. I fix your lunch and you watch television. I take . . ."

"All right, all right," yelled an angry Bart as he stomped into the kitchen. "I'll do it, I'll do it." He picked up the trash can, opened the back door, and after checking to make sure his mother wasn't watching, set the trash on the first step below the door. Then he came back in and resumed watching television.

Primary Problem: No specific job description has been established, no schedule has been set for taking out the kitchen trash, and no direction is given until Christa loses her temper and screams, "Take out the trash right now." Mom never actually told Bart to take out the trash. She reminded him about the trash ("Don't forget the trash, honey"). She made an observation about the trash ("The trash is still waiting"). She asked him when he was going to "get the trash." And she asked him about his plans for the trash ("Just how long do you plan on leaving the trash overflowing onto the floor?"). But until she got angry and followed through, she didn't direct him to take out the trash And if children aren't clearly directed to do something ("Clean your room" or "Feed the dog" or "Finish your homework") and told when to do it ("Now" or "As soon as dinner is over" or "At three o'clock"), they usually won't do it. And if the task isn't scheduled ("Every day at 9:00 P.M." or "Every night as soon as dinner is over" or "As soon as you get home from school every day"), children will not habituate the schedule and will continue to wait for you to make them do it.

Perhaps you are saying to yourself, "Why should I have to go into that kind of detail for a teenager who knows what I want?" But the truth of the matter is that when it comes to doing tasks we dislike, many of us do as little as we can get by with. Virtually every business, government agency, school, and church has to write out detailed job descriptions for its adult workers. Businesses pay attorneys billions of dollars a year to write (or to subvert) contracts that spell out in detail how and when all of the *adults* who are parties to those contracts are to behave. McDonald's 600-page operations manual describes in the smallest detail how to do every job in the restaurant, when to do it, and how often to do it. McDonald's, Taco Bell, and other fast-food restaurants spend millions of dollars a year on training videos and require that their employees watch the videos until they can do their jobs just like the people in the videos do.

The Solution: If America's corporations, small businesses, government agencies, schools, and churches all need detailed job descriptions to make sure the adults in their employ do their jobs properly, doesn't it make sense that children, who frequently don't want the jobs parents give them, need comprehensive job descriptions too? Job descriptions are also good for parents in that they force us to examine and clarify exactly what we want our children to do.

CLEARLY DEFINING THE RULES

When is the kitchen trash can full enough to be taken out? Is it full when the first piece of trash sits above the top of the can? Is it full when no more trash can be put in the can? Or is it full when the first piece of trash rolls off the can and onto the floor? What if a child stomps the trash halfway down into the can? Is it still full? What if the child sets a paper grocery bag next to the full trash can to receive the overflow? Is the trash full enough to take out now? And even if the definition of "full" could be clearly established, what are the children to do if they aren't in the room when the trash can becomes full, or aren't even home when it becomes full? And if the trash is no longer "full" but is "overflowing," does it still have to be taken out?

The Solution: A rule that requires children to take out the trash "whenever it's full" doesn't have a structure that can be reinforced. Unless the rule is clarified, made more specific, and most important, put on a schedule, getting children to take out full cans of trash will require never-ending parent reminders for years to come. Always be as specific as the child needs. Put all continuing household duties, including studying and doing homework, on a regular schedule.

SETTING AND ENFORCING SCHEDULES

Task-oriented rules that don't include schedules train children to procrastinate and to put off doing their chores until forced to do so. In fact, in many households parents have told their youngsters hundreds of times, over many years, to take the trash out, but even though the "kids" are now in their twenties, Mom or Dad still must say, "Take out the trash *now*," because they have never established a schedule for taking out the trash. Even comparatively easy-to-raise children will rarely assume responsibility for household chores and tasks without being trained to follow a schedule. And temperamentally difficult children will never assume responsibility for doing household chores, tasks, or homework without being trained to a schedule.

The Solution: Instead of just saying, "Take out the trash now," establish a schedule that includes specifically what is to be done ("Take all of the trash out to the curb"), when it is to be done ("now and right after dinner"), how often it is to be done ("every Friday night"), and how long the task is to be done ("from now on"). "Take all of the trash out to the curb now and every Friday night right after dinner from now on."

SPECIFYING WHO IS TO DO THE JOB

A hopeful, optimistic mom called from work, as she did most days, and talked to her three children on the kitchen speakerphone shortly after they got home from school. She reminded them that "Somebody had better clean up the kitchen, including the trash, and take care of the dogs, before I get home." But since no one named "somebody" lived in the home, the kitchen was still dirty, the trash was more than full, and the backyard was littered with dog waste when Mom got home.

Many parents don't consistently specify who is to do what, and then they wonder why their kids never do anything without being yelled at. But the truth of the matter is simple: you can't count on children to offer to do unpleasant jobs on their own. "Oh, Mom, I know no one else wants to do it, so while my sisters are watching television I'll clean the kitchen, take out the trash, and clean up after the dogs." Right.

The Solution: Always be specific about who is to do what jobs. No positive structure can be built on children's behavioral templates until their specific duties are properly assigned.

BLAME AND PERSONAL CRITICISM DAMAGE STRUCTURE

If a parent focuses on a child as "the problem" ("You are inconsiderate and selfish" or "You are lazy and good for nothing" or "You don't care about anybody but yourself"), the rules for cleaning up the kitchen, throwing dirty clothes into the hamper, hanging up clean clothes, and coming home on time tend to get lost in arguments, accusations, attacks, defensiveness, and counterattacks. The same is true when children focus on their parents as "the problem" ("You make me do everything"; "None of the other mothers are as mean as you"; "You treat me like a baby").

To avoid dealing with children as problems, many therapists tell parents to switch the focus from "you" statements to "I" statements, apparently without recognizing that "I" statements still focus on a person as the problem. So instead of saying, "You will take out the trash right now," which truly is provocative, parents are instructed to say, "It bothers me when you don't take out the trash, as you promised" (Gee, that's too bad, Mom. Why don't you talk to your shrink about it?"). While it may be less threatening, this is certainly more patronizing. Look at one of the recommended examples from *Parent Effectiveness Training (P.E.T.)*, where a child "comes to the table with very dirty hands and face" and his father says, "I can't enjoy my dinner when I see all that dirt. It makes me feel kind of sick and I lose my appetite" (p. 132). Contrast that statement with this one, where the parent stays focused on the rule about washing before meals: "Honey, come into the bathroom with me so you can wash up for dinner. From now on, just before you eat, come to the bathroom and wash your face and hands with a wet washcloth and soap until all the dirt is gone. Then dry yourself off with the hand towel, wring out the washcloth, fold it and the towel neatly, and put them back on the towel bar. Do this every time just before you eat from now on. And for the next week or two, we'll do this together." In this example the father stays focused on the task at hand (washing the hands and face); he monitors and follows through as necessary, and he is consistent—rather than complaining that his son's dirty face and hands make him feel sick.

Never focus on a person as a problem, and don't allow anyone, especially your children, to focus on you as a problem. Always concentrate on the task to be completed or the rule to be followed. You may, however, focus on people, especially your children and spouse, when you are telling them how nice they look, how pretty a new hairstyle looks, what a good job they did in the yard, and how much you love them.

5
PROVOCATION AND MANIPULATION

From an early age, difficult children habituate the skills to challenge, manipulate, and provoke parents and others to get their way, or they find loopholes that allow them to evade unpleasant tasks. Some of these techniques are relatively harmless and end in childhood; others, if unchecked, can lead to a lifetime of belligerence and violence, befouling and destroying relationship after relationship at school, at home, and on the job.

Discussed below are the most commonly practiced challenges, manipulations, and provocations used by children to get their way. Please keep in mind that the child's objective in using these techniques is always the same: to take control of an unfavorable situation by changing the topic, misdirecting the parent's attention, or escalating the level of anger. Even though they frequently complain to the contrary, difficult children don't really care if parents are fair, reasonable, logical, or caring. They don't actually care if parents are old-fashioned ("This isn't the 1960s, you know") or are from another country ("This is America, not Vietnam"), or are older ("You're the oldest mother I know"), or are divorced ("If you hadn't left Dad, everything would be fine"). All that matters to difficult-to-discipline children is that they get their way right now and, short of that goal, that they at least be able to maintain control of the situations in which they find themselves.

Here are the most common provocations and manipulations used by children against parents, teachers, and other adult authority figures. Each one is followed by advice on how to control it.

Arguing

If arguing were an Olympic sport most temperamentally difficult children would be medal contenders.

DEFLECTING AND SPONGING

Instead of arguing or responding to children's oral provocations, deflect arguments with the words "regardless" and "nevertheless." And for those children who must have the last word at all costs, stop the argument by "sponging" them with these words and phrases: "Uh-huh," "I heard you," "Anything else?" and "You already said that."

The examples below demonstrate the wrong way and right way to deal with an argumentative child.

THE COMPARER: CHILD IN CONTROL

"Ramon, please pick up your dirty clothes and put them in the hamper," Mom said as she walked by fourteen-year-old Ramon, who was playing a video game.

"Why do you always pick on me? You never make Lisa do anything around here," Ramon said while he continued to play the game.

"That's not true, and you know it," said Mom. "She has more to do around here than you do."

"Oh, right, Mom. And the Easter Bunny really brings candy and eggs to all the little children."

"You'd better watch that smart mouth of yours, Ramon Alberto Ruiz. I won't put up with it."

"Oh, it's always my mouth that needs to be watched. Lisa never says anything bad, does she?" asked Ramon, continuing to play the video game while arguing. He never does get up and put his dirty clothes in the hamper.

THE COMPARER: PARENT IN CONTROL

"Ramon, please pick up your dirty clothes and put them in the hamper," Mom said as she walked by fourteen-year-old Ramon, who was playing a video game.

"Why do you always pick on me? You never make Lisa do anything around here," Ramon said while he continued to play the game.

*"**Regardless** of what Lisa does, pick up your dirty clothes and put them in the hamper," said Mom, turning off the game.*

"That's not fair. You wouldn't turn off the TV on Lisa," said Ramon.

*"**Regardless** of whether it's fair or not, put your clothes in the hamper right now," said Mom, watching Ramon as he went to put his dirty clothes in the hamper.*

See how much better that went? Tempers were cooler, and the job got done right away. The only thing Mom could have done better was to set up a continuing rule requiring Ramon always to put his dirty clothes in the hamper as soon as he took them off.

THE SUBJECT CHANGER: CHILD IN CONTROL

"Clint," Mom said as her thirteen-year-old son walked out the front door to shoot some hoops in a brand-new expensive shirt. "That shirt cost too much for you to play in it. Put on an old one."

"It was on sale, Mom," said Clint, irritated. "And besides, I paid for part of it."

"You haven't given me any money for it yet."

"Mom," said Clint, releasing a big sigh and contorting his body in exasperation, "why do you always do this? I was feeling fine, but you have to go and ruin everything."

Mom said angrily. "How have I done that?"

"You're always on my back about something. You never can let me be," he continued, ready to thrust his hurtful words into the most vulnerable part of her heart. "You drove Dad away by doing the same thing to him."

"You know that isn't true," said Mom, emotionally overwhelmed with pain.

"Have it your way, Mom," Clint said as he walked out the door wearing his brand-new shirt.

THE SUBJECT CHANGER: PARENT IN CONTROL

"Clint," Mom said as her thirteen-year-old son walked out the front door to shoot some hoops in a brand-new expensive shirt. "That shirt cost too much for you to play in it. Put on an old one."

"It was on sale, Mom," said Clint, irritated. "And besides, I paid for part of it."

*"**Regardless**, go change your shirt now."*

"Mom," said Clint, releasing a big sigh and contorting his body in exasperation, "why do you always do this? I was feeling fine, but you have to go and ruin everything."

*"**Nevertheless**, go change your shirt now."*

"You're really getting mean."

*"**Regardless** of whether I'm mean or not, go change your shirt right now," Mom said as she escorted Clint to his bedroom and watched him change his shirt.*

This time Mom stuck to the main issue all the way through until the shirt was changed. She deflected Clint's provocations and returned to the subject at hand. The only element she needed to add was a rule requiring that Clint never go out and play in new clothes.

THE BADGERER: CHILD IN CONTROL

Mom was bent over, sorting the wash when sixteen-year-old Jenny walked into the laundry room and asked, "Can I spend the night at Linda's after tonight's basketball game?"

"Linda who?" asked Mom.

"Linda Reese. You've met her. She was in my English class."

"When did I meet her? What does she look like?"

"God, Mom!" said Jenny, rolling her eyes. "Do you want her finger-prints and Social Security number, too?"

"Sounds good to me," said Mom, standing up to start the washing machine. "Just tell me who she is."

"The one you saw in the car with Bobbie a couple of weeks ago," added Jenny, exasperated.

"The one dressed in black with the sides of her head shaved? The one smoking a cigarette? The one with the filthy mouth? You've got to be kidding. There's no way I'd let you go over there," said Mom, bending over to pull dry clothes out of the dryer.

"But why? You don't even know her."

"You're right. I don't know her, but I know enough to say you can't go."

"That's not fair."

"I don't care if it's fair or not," said Mom, exasperated, as she folded the

clean laundry. You can't spend the night at Linda's or with anyone else I don't know."

"Why?"

"Because I don't want you spending the night with people I'm not comfortable with."

"But that's stupid. Why can't I go?"

"I told you why," said Mom, getting angry.

"But that's stupid. So why can't I go?"

"I don't want you to get into trouble," yelled Mom.

"You don't trust me?" You think I'm going to get into trouble? I don't believe you. I'm sixteen years old and you're trying to tell me who I can be friends with. What's wrong with you?"

Mom picked up the basket of folded clothes and walked away without responding.

"Don't walk away from me. I'm still talking to you," Jenny yelled indignantly as she followed her mother into the hallway. "Why can't I go to Linda's?"

"I told you why. Now leave me alone," said Mom, placing towels and sheets in the linen closet.

"Give me a good reason," Jenny said aggressively.

Mom threw the laundry basket on the floor and screamed, "Leave me alone!"

"Not until you give me a good reason why I can't spend the night at Linda's," said Jenny, grabbing her mother's wrist.

Mom wrenched her arm away from Jenny's grasp and quickly walked to the kitchen in a futile attempt to get away.

Jenny pursued Mom, still demanding, "Why can't I go?"

Mom braced herself against the kitchen counter and said, "Okay, I give up. Go. Do whatever you want. Just leave me alone and get out of here."

THE BADGERER: PARENT IN CONTROL

Mom was bent over, sorting the wash when sixteen-year-old Jenny walked into the laundry room and asked, "Can I spend the night at Linda's after tonight's basketball game?"

"Linda who?" asked Mom.

"Linda Reese. You've met her. She was in my English class."

"When did I meet her? What does she look like?"

"God, Mom!" said Jenny, rolling her eyes. "Do you want her fingerprints and Social Security number, too."

"Sounds good to me," said Mom, standing up to start the washing machine. "Just tell me who she is."

"The one you saw in the car with Bobbie a couple of weeks ago," added Jenny, exasperated."

"The one dressed in black with the sides of her head shaved? The one smoking a cigarette? The one with the filthy mouth? You've got to be kidding. There's no way I'd let you go over there," said Mom, bending over to pull dry clothes out of the dryer.

"But why? You don't even know her."

"*Regardless* of why, you may not go."

[Mom, in asking her questions about the girl's shaved head, her smoking, and her filthy mouth, has through implication, clearly let Jenny know what the problem is. Also, Mom knows that Jenny is a badgerer and that no matter what she says, Jenny will have a belligerent, provocative response.]

"You don't trust me, do you?" asked Jenny, putting her hands on her hips and staring at Mom.

"*Regardless* of whether I trust you or not, you may not go," said Mom, continuing to work.

"All the other mothers are letting their daughters go," said Jenny, trying a different tack.

"*Uh-huh*," said Mom, sponging up Jenny's provocation.

Jenny paused momentarily, not sure how to continue. "Well, they are. The other parents are letting their daughters go."

"*You already said that*, honey," Mom said, leaving the laundry room.

"Well, can I go?"

"No." Mom walked into the bathroom and closed the door behind her.

"But why?"

"*Regardless* of why, you may not go," Mom replied through the bathroom door.

"I hate the word 'regardless.' "

"*Nevertheless*," you may not go.

Jenny stomped off, not quite sure what had happened.

This time Mom stuck to the main issue. No matter how hard Jenny attempted to provoke her, she deflected the provocations and got right back to the subject at hand.

PROVOCATIVE SWEARING: CHILD IN CONTROL

Mom was coming into the apartment with her arms full of groceries when fourteen-year-old Lee Ann hung up the telephone and started to leave. As usual, she was dressed in her skinhead gear, including Doc Martins — the English shoes favored by punks, skinheads, and other "alternative kids" — jeans, a white T-shirt, and a civil air patrol flight jacket. Her blond hair was skinned at the sides.

"Where are you going?" asked Mom, putting the bags down.

"Out," replied Lee Ann, standing halfway between Mom and the doorway.

"Out where?"

"It's none of your business."

"Yes, it is my business. Now, where are you going?"

"Fuck you!" Lee Ann said contemptuously.

Mom took a long step and looked Lee Ann in the eye. "Don't you ever talk to me that way."

"What are you going to do, hit me? Go ahead, bitch. Hit me. I'll report you for child abuse."

"Don't talk to me that way, ever."

"Fuck you, bitch."

Mom slapped Lee Ann sharply across the face. "I won't tolerate that language in my house, especially from a child."

Lee Ann put her finger to her tongue. A small speck of blood was visible on the tip of her finger. "Look what you did!"

"You must have caught your braces against the side of your mouth when I slapped you. I'm sorry you're hurt, honey, but you can't swear at me."

"Bullshit. I'm reporting you for child abuse." And as she walked out the door she gave her Mom one more shot. "Fuck you, bitch. You aren't going to keep me from seeing my friends."

PROVOCATIVE SWEARING: PARENT IN CONTROL

Mom was coming into the apartment with her arms full of groceries when Lee Ann hung up the telephone and started to leave.

"Where are you going?" asked Mom, putting the bags down.

"Out," replied Lee Ann, standing halfway between Mom and the doorway.

"Out where?"

"It's none of your business."

*"**Regardless** of whether it's my business or not, where are you going?"*

"Fuck you!" Lee Ann said contemptuously.

*Mom took two long steps and stood in front of the door. "**Uh-huh**," Mom sponged, not about to engage in an argument or to let Lee Ann leave.*

"Are you fucking deaf?" screamed Lee Ann.

*"Lee Ann," said Mom calmly, "**regardless** of how many times you say 'fuck,' you may not leave home tonight."*

"Fuck you, bitch."

*"**Anything else**?" Mom asked as she watched Lee Ann stomp off to her room.*

Lee Ann was not allowed to take control in the second episode. Mom stayed focused on the main issue. No matter how hard Lee Ann attempted to provoke her, Mom deflected her provocations and got back to the matter at hand. The only element that still needs to be resolved is Lee Ann's disrespect and foul language, and the more consistent Mom and Dad are over the next few weeks in following the program set out in this book, the less disrespectful and provocative she will be.

Arguing is one of the most effective techniques children can use to control their parents and other adults. It is also one of the most dangerous practices within a family. Almost all family violence starts with arguing, including fights between parents and children and fights between Mom and Dad. And many children habituate arguing on their behavioral templates at an early age to use against family members now and into the future for decades to come.

The Solution: Never argue with a child. You can't win. The best you can hope for is an energy-sapping, emotionally wrenching tie. Instead of arguing, reread the examples above, out loud, over and over until sponging and deflecting become a habit. Also, consistently practice deflecting and sponging children's arguments with your spouse, relatives, and friends. Of all the things you can do to take control of your children's provocations and manipulations, nothing is more effective than deflecting and sponging arguments.

Lying

Except for those children who tell grandiose lies ("The Dodgers asked me to pitch for them this year"), lying is rarely a primary problem. The actual problem is the misbehavior the child is trying to cover up with the lie. Lying is almost always used either to cover up misbehavior or to provoke an argument. So instead of arguing with your children about whether or not they are telling the truth, always stay focused on their misbehavior by using deflectors and sponges.

THE BLATANT LIAR: CHILD IN CONTROL

Justin, sixteen years old, and Isaac, age thirteen, were watching television in the family room. Just as Dad walked in, Justin reached over and punched Isaac hard on the shoulder with his fist.

"Hey, knock it off," Dad yelled.

"Knock what off?" asked Justin as he turned and looked at Dad.

"Don't hit your brother. Don't be a bully."

"I didn't hit anyone," protested Justin.

"Justin, I saw you hit him."

"No, you didn't. You couldn't have because I didn't hit him."

"Now, quit it. I saw you hit Isaac. Admit it."

"There's nothing to admit. I didn't do anything wrong."

"Don't lie to me," screamed Dad.

"I'm not lying," screamed Justin, standing up and facing his father. "You never believe me."

"That's because you're always lying."

"Fine," yelled Justin, reversing fields and catching Dad off guard. "You win. I'm a liar. I hit Isaac."

"That's right, you did," said Dad, unsure of himself.

"Of course. I confess," Justin said sarcastically.

"I give up," said Dad, and walked away.

Justin sat back down on the couch, reached over, and slugged Isaac on the shoulder with his fist.

THE BLATANT LIAR: PARENT IN CONTROL

Justin, sixteen years old, and Isaac, age thirteen, were watching television in the family room. Just as Dad walked in, Justin reached over and punched Isaac hard on the shoulder with his fist.

"Stop it, Justin. Never hit your brother again," Dad said firmly.

"I didn't hit anyone," protested Justin.

"**Regardless**, never hit your brother."

"But I didn't hit him!"

"**Nevertheless**, don't ever do it."

"I didn't do anything wrong."

"**You've already said that**," said Dad sponging up the argument. "And, Justin, until I can count on you to leave your brother alone, you can stay with me outside while I work in the yard."

"That's not fair."

"**Nevertheless**, come outside with me now," said Dad, escorting Justin into the backyard.

Lying is one of the most powerful manipulative devices children can use to control their parents. At the minimum, it either distracts parents from the real issues at hand and focuses their attention on the secondary issue of lying or it leads parents into the chaos of arguing.

The Solution: Never argue with a child about a lie. You rarely win. Instead of arguing, learn to deflect and sponge arguments about lies. Only after you are completely through dealing with the primary misbehavior should you come back and lay down a rule against lying.

Threatening

Threats, more than anything else, are argument provocations. Whether the children threaten to kill themselves, to run away, or to go live with their other divorced parent, never give in to the provocation, and never argue.

The Solution: Use deflectors and sponges to stay in control of the situation: "**Regardless** of whether you kill yourself or not, you may not go to the party with your friends." "**Regardless** of whether you'll run away or not, you will start attending your new school on Monday." "**Nevertheless**, clean your room now and every Saturday morning at eight o'clock from now on."

If you are worried about children's threats to harm themselves, don't take chances. Depending on their apparent level of sincerity, call 911 in critical cases and report that your child is talking of suicide. In less critical situations, promptly schedule a psychological evaluation. If you aren't sure how serious the threat may be, at the minimum do what the professional staff in psychiatric hospitals do to ensure that suicide risks don't harm themselves: supervise the child closely until the threat is over.

Throwing a Temper Tantrum

Some temperamentally difficult children use anger as a weapon to control their parents. Most, however, have simply never been structured to control their temper. But regardless of whether tantrums are used with purpose and forethought, or out of frustration at not getting one's way, the sooner they are brought under control, the better.

The Solution: Since most temper tantrums start during an argument, never argue with a child. Instead, as noted above, deflect or sponge your children's argument provocations. If you still find yourself with an angry, out-of-control child, use a time-out to calm him or her down.

Time-out starts with a quiet place where there is nothing to do except calm down. Good places for time-outs include entryways, empty corners, and staircases. As soon as children start to lose control, send them to a time-out, and keep them there until they have calmed down and are ready to comply with your rules. No talking, yelling, screaming, singing, howling, bird noises, burping, or passing gas for at least five minutes. Nor may they leave the time-out area for at least five minutes. If they do, or if they talk or make any noise in the first five minutes, the time-out starts all over again. They may wind up spending thirty to forty minutes or longer in time-outs the first few times this is done; but if this approach is used consistently, they will throw fewer tantrums, and those that do occur will become progressively shorter. Use time-outs until you no longer need to use them. The time-out is not a form of punishment, and if it is used for more than providing the time and space to calm down, or as a place for warring siblings to calm down, it won't work to change behavior.

No doubt some of you are thinking, Sure. I'm going to put an angry 160-pound kid, who's punching holes in the wall and calling me a "fucking bitch," into the corner. How? Read the following section on controlling violent children.

Violence

Just in case you have any doubt, violence—especially violence directed at parents—is a watershed behavior that cannot be tolerated. Children who learn to get their way through the use of physical intimidation and violence are potentially dangerous to everyone. Additionally, children who batter their parents are at risk for committing every kind of violent criminal behavior, including rape, robbery, battery, spouse and child abuse, and murder.

Some children are violent because at some point early in their lives they discovered that their parents had no idea how to deal with their tantrums, and they decided to capitalize on that fact. Others found their parents to be passive and unwilling to confront their tantrums. Or they took up with destructive friends—street gangs, skinheads, punks, heavy metalers, and other alternative kids—who assumed a violent antiauthoritarian position against everyone in authority, including parents. But the most dangerous children are boys who have been raised in chaotic homes with passive, submissive mothers and violent men. When these boys don't get their way, it is not unusual for them to take over where Mom's battering ex-husband or ex-boyfriend left off. And in some families, once an older child hits Mom or uses physical intimidation to get his or her way, the younger children will follow suit.

The Solution: If the situation is critical, and your children threaten you with a weapon or beat you up, do whatever is necessary to protect yourself and immediately call the police. Don't take any chances. Once the situation is temporarily stabilized and the personal safety of those in your home is assured, you have several alternatives to choose from. As a first choice, consider sending the child to a highly structured, well-supervised wilderness program. Such a program, combined with a solidly structured parent-training program, can calm and restructure all but the most violent children. Residential treatment programs and psychiatric centers can also help violent children control their tempers and fists. Finally, in some situations you may be forced to use the juvenile court and the institutions and programs at its disposal. Unfortunately, however, wilderness therapy and especially residential treatment programs and psychiatric centers are very expensive, and the juvenile court, if it is even willing to work with you, can limit your parental authority. If you don't have the financial resources to pay for private assistance, or if you don't wish to lose your parental authority, you must learn how to control your child's temper tantrums and violence directly.

If you are a parent with no other resource or assistance, and you have a violent teenager—one who smacks you around, slugs you, kicks you, throws you against the wall or down on the floor—it is imperative that you learn to defend yourself. Enroll in a self-defense class or, better yet, take private lessons from a self-defense instructor in pins, holds, and restraints. You don't need a black belt in one of the martial arts to protect yourself. And you clearly don't want to learn to maim or disable your violent child. Instead, you need to be trained by a qualified self-defense instructor to do the basic pins, holds, and restraints that police officers, psychiatric hospital staff, and juvenile hall counselors use to protect themselves and the violent children with whom they have to work.

With consistent practice you can learn how to put violent children on the floor and keep them there until they have calmed down and are willing to go to a time-out to finish the calming process, as described above. Interestingly, the majority of the parents who take self-defense lessons never need to use what they have learned. The more confident they become in dealing with their out-of-control children, the less often their children challenge them physically.

For smaller violent children who can still be physically restrained, either sit them in your lap or place them chest down on the floor, depending on their size, and wrap your arms around them in a firm bear hug, using your legs to pin their legs together. If he or she must be placed on the floor, your body weight must be centered on the child's hips and thighs. Never put your body weight on the child's chest. If the child is also swearing, screaming, calling you names, or making threats, use one hand to hold his hands together at the wrists and use your other hand to cover his mouth, cupping your hand so it can't be bitten. Softly saying into the child's ear, "As soon as you calm down and are ready to stop hitting [or kicking or biting], I'll let you go to time-out. Calm down, honey. Calm down. I love you. As soon as you're ready to . . ."

Don't let the child out of your bear hug, though, until his or her muscles and voice completely relax. The first time you do this, it may take anywhere from five to more than sixty minutes for the child finally to calm down. Repeat this process every time the child throws an aggressive tantrum or is violent. The more consistently you use the bear hug for violent tantrums, the more your children will learn to control their frustration and their temper tantrums. For most children—even uncooperative, temperamentally difficult children—the safest, most comforting place to be when they are upset is in Mom or Dad's arms.

6

FLAWED SUPERVISION: PARENT OUT OF CONTROL

ℭℰ

Peer Cultures, Social Cliques, and Bonded Relationships

All people, including children, are social creatures. The same conforming social and emotional forces within the ethological milieus that structure the hearts and minds of newborn children to become Japanese or Serbian, Basque or Hasidim, Zulu or Amish, American working class or underclass can also structure children to become delinquents, stoners, punks, or gangsters.

The most dangerous enemies your children may ever face are sometimes their friends, associates, and others with whom they bond emotionally. Most temperamentally difficult children are already burdened with a tendency toward impulsiveness and emotionally based decision-making. They generally act on how they feel at the moment, and they rarely think about the possible consequences of their behavior. As a result, they are especially vulnerable to the excitement, fun, and exhilaration frequently associated with kids who live on or beyond the edge. They also enjoy the sense of power and control over others that comes with being a member of a delinquent or rebellious subculture or gang.

Tragically, many parents underestimate the power of children's attachment and bonding to destructive peers. Fewer yet are aware of the incredible influence of corrupt child-based cultures like street gangs and bands of skinheads. As a result, they fail to adequately supervise their children's friends, whereabouts, and activities. They

76

don't monitor clothing, hairstyles, or musical preferences. Many parents also allow their children to be in highly tempting, provocative situations and expect them to exercise good judgment and not react to strong emotional stimuli—going to unsupervised parties and not using alcohol or drugs, dating steadily and not becoming emotionally or sexually involved, or associating with destructive peers and not taking on their values and behavior patterns. Placing children in these situations is like sending alcoholics to a bar, overeaters to a bakery, or politicians to a cash-laden lobbyist and expecting them not to drink, eat, or take the cash.

Almost all kids are heavily influenced by child-based cultures that establish values, behavior standards, clothing styles, and attitudes toward school, family, alcohol, drugs, sex, and even crime. And when children's behavioral templates are structured by other kids, they incorporate the immature values of their friends within their character. *Just one negative friend to whom the child has become emotionally bonded can undo everything that good, loving parents have accomplished.*

Many of America's increasing number of "lost children" are morally corrupted, emotionally handicapped, or psychologically damaged during their teen and even preteen years, largely because of their bonded relationships with damaged, delinquent, or otherwise dangerous children and the child-based cultures to which they belong.

When Children Raise Children

Responsible adult supervision, especially parental supervision, is essential in building strong, honorable, and dependable structures. American teenagers are at highest risk for most of life's dangers at a time in their lives when they are least likely to be supervised by adults. Most children under the age of thirteen are still accountable to adults almost all of the time. Most adults, regardless of their age, are also accountable to someone—spouses, employers, co-workers, friends, and even their children—almost all of the time. But most teenagers, and unfortunately a growing number of their younger siblings, are spending increasingly more time in the company of other children, away from all aspects of responsible adult supervision—and all of us, especially the kids, are paying the price. And the phenomenon of children raising children, which is common throughout the nation, is seen most often and most destructively in America's inner cities.

Leon Dash, a reporter for the *Washington Post*, spent a year in an impoverished neighborhood in Washington, D.C., that has one of the nation's highest unmarried teenage birth rates. (*When Children Want Children, The Urban Crisis of Teenage Childbearing*, 1989.) He talked to kids and to their parents, grandparents, great-grandparents, and neighbors. He unexpectedly found that most of the children, even young children, knew about birth control and clearly understood how the different methods of birth control worked. In every instance of pregnancy, he found that at least one of the parties involved actually *wanted* a baby, primarily because of a strong young-male peer culture that declared boys to be men when they produced babies, and a separate but equally powerful young-female peer culture that declared girls to be worthless if they couldn't make babies. One of the worst put-downs a girl can receive in this neighborhood is to be taunted with the charge that she is "barren." The vast majority of middle-class teenage girls, black or white, wouldn't even know what "barren" means, let alone be offended or challenged by it. But it's enough to provoke a heated fight in this part of Washington.

Dash found that the cultural values that encourage young girls in the inner city to have babies came from the earliest days of sharecropping and that those cultural values are passed on by children's peers, not by their parents. But Dash also identified a contemporary destructive parenting practice that was likewise developed during the sharecropping era, where parents give their older children the responsibility of supervising the younger children in the home or in the neighborhood. Just as their great-grandparents did more than sixty years ago when they went out to tend the crops, it is common for inner-city mothers today to send young children outside to play for hours at a time on the common grounds and streets of dangerous neighborhoods, supervised only by older children. As a result, many inner-city children are raised in an ethological milieu where the values, attitudes, and behavior patterns of America's meanest streets are enforced by the toughest kids in the neighborhood.

Twenty years earlier, Arthur Hippler found the same cultural practices in use, with the same destructive results, almost three thousand miles away, in the Hunter's Point housing project in San Francisco (*Hunter's Point: A Black Ghetto*, 1974). And Eugene D. Genovese, going back to the eighteenth and early nineteenth century, found identical customs recorded in the diaries and journals of slaves and others (*Roll, Jordan, Roll*, 1974). Even though they serve no contemporary use, even though they are highly destructive to the people involved, chaos-producing child-rearing practices and sex-related values that originated in the slavery and sharecropping eras are still being passed on to new behavioral templates, generation to generation, by the children of the urban poor.

Dangerous and callous sexual attitudes, however, aren't limited to kids in the inner city. In the greater New York City area, reporters for the *New York Times* found widespread contempt for girls by boys who demonstrate their manhood to their friends by "abusing or showing disrespect to girls." They also found that "a growing number seem to view sexual harassment as a game, and abuse as a team sport." And perhaps, most disturbing, these boys purposely refuse to establish caring relationships with or emotional attachments to girls. To do so would be seen as a sign of weakness within the ethological milieu of those teenage boys: "The guys don't want to look soft to their friends" (*New York Times*, July 11, 1993, p. 1). The longer those boys spend in that social environment, the more ingrained those attitudes will become, and the greater will be the likelihood of more out-of-marriage babies being born to fathers who won't take care of them.

And this problem is not confined to the East Coast. In suburban Lakewood, California, more than two dozen poorly supervised teenage boys calling themselves the Spur Posse, formed a clique with a primary goal of seeing who could sexually "score" with the most girls. Points were given for every new conquest. The age, looks, weight, and personality of the girls were immaterial. Most of the boys held the girls in contempt, calling them sluts and pigs. Many of the girls, who were also poorly supervised, were passed around from boy to boy. Others made themselves available for "gang bangs" with eight or more boys in succession ("Hanging with the Spur Posse," *Rolling Stone*, July 8–22, 1993). And as younger boys and girls joined the gang or its harem, the values, attitudes, and behavior of the older kids were built on the new kids' behavioral templates for future use.

In addition to sexual values, delinquent and criminal peer cultures are also passed from older child to younger child and from generation to generation. By reviewing decades of court records in Chicago, researchers Clifford Shaw and Henry McKay found a constant pattern of older and younger boys linked together in crime "backward in time in an unbroken continuity" (*Juvenile Delinquency and Urban Areas*, revised edition, 1969). Most of the chaos normally associated with poorly supervised, poorly structured children—crime and violence, drugs, gangs, early sex, dropping out of school—is rapidly cascading through America from child to child via friendships, peer cliques, delinquent and criminal subcultures, and corrupt media-sponsored youth cultures.

Virtually all tobacco smokers start smoking after they regularly associate with other smokers. The average age at which they start smoking is twelve. Comparatively few smokers start smoking past the age of twenty-one. Most young smokers use tobacco when unsupervised by responsible adults.

Virtually all drug users start using drugs after they regularly associate with other drug users. The vast majority of drug users start using drugs before they are twenty-one years old. Almost all drug use by children takes place when children are unsupervised by responsible adults.

Most runaways don't start running away from home until after they start regularly associating with children who have a history of running away, or with others who support and encourage running away. Runaways are almost always marginally supervised by responsible adults.

Students with a long history of academic success who suddenly stop studying, stop doing their homework, stop participating in classroom activities, and stop being a part of the school community almost always have started regularly associating with one or more peers who are also failing at school.

Most truants start cutting classes and leaving school only after they regularly associate with other truants. On-campus truancy and class-cutting can take place only on campuses with inadequate adult supervision.

Most teenage alcohol abusers start abusing alcohol when they regularly associate with other alcohol abusers. Much of that abuse takes places at teenage parties that are poorly supervised or unsupervised by responsible adults.

In addition to their actual peers, many children emotionally bond to corrupt media-sponsored youth-culture icons. Hundreds of thousands of teenagers and preteens have bonded with the peer-culture heroes of heavy metal, gangster rap, and punk bands. (There are even underground bands that cater to skinheads.) The teenagers dress like these pop idols, act like them, talk like them, share their values and attitudes, and wear identical clothes, jewelry, hairstyles, and footwear. Teenage heavy metalers feel that they are directly linked to Metallica, or Guns N' Roses. Young street gangsters and hundreds of thousands of wanna-bes feel that groups like Public Enemy and N.W.A. (Niggers With Attitude) are a part of the same gang culture that they belong to—and they're right. Bands that publicly live and participate in "outlaw" peer cultures provide their fans with a sense of identity, power, and belonging.

Children who start identifying with these outlaws typically incorporate negative peer-culture values, behavior patterns, and beliefs on their behavioral templates and start to behave badly at home. Many children join these peer cultures solely because they have emotionally bonded with bands proselytizing for converts. Most, however, have one or more friends who are also involved in an outlaw peer culture.

Because of inadequate supervision, American teenagers lead the world by a wide margin in virtually every negative category. America has the world's greatest number of teenage unwed mothers, many of whom will raise their children in a lifetime of poverty. American teenagers are the world's busiest killers. They are also more likely to be murdered than anyone else in America. American teenage girls are more likely to be raped than any other group of women in the world. Half of America's criminals are twenty-one years old or younger. And American teenagers are the victims of criminals more than any other age group in the country. By the age of eighteen, 80 percent of America's teenagers admit to drinking to drunkenness, and more than 25 percent admit to using drugs regularly. Some 80 percent of the crime on American college and university campuses is committed by young students against other young students—on campuses where, "After 10:00 P.M., the campus with its wild drinking and reckless sex, is almost entirely adultless" ("The Ivory Tower Becomes an Armed Camp," *New York Times Magazine*, March 7, 1993).

If your children's social clique (the specific group of friends and associates to whom the child is bonded) or peer culture (a clearly identifiable peer social system that can be as small as a social clique or as large as all of the people who identify themselves as skinheads, heavy metalers, or punks) values the regular use of drugs, alcohol, or tobacco, the likelihood that they use drugs, alcohol, or tobacco is almost 100 percent. And the longer they are a part of that social clique or peer culture, the stronger they will habituate the use of drugs, alcohol, and tobacco. If the group values criminal behavior, the likelihood that they will participate in criminal activity is extremely high. And the longer they are a part of a criminal value system, the greater the likelihood of long-term criminality.

So it comes down to this: since the structure with which they enter adulthood will in large part determine how well they live their lives, whom do you want to structure your children's behavioral templates for drug use, crime, gang membership, school, sex, and work habits?

Structuring Agents: Parents and Other Adults or Unsupervised Peers?

DRUGS, ALCOHOL, AND TOBACCO

Unsupervised Peers: The more time children spend with their friends and associates, in person and on the telephone, away from responsible adult supervision, the greater the risk for all types of chemical involvement, especially if any of their associates are drug, alcohol, or tobacco users. If the children are temperamentally difficult, the risk is even greater.

Parents, Adults, and Supervised Peers: The more time children spend with their parents and other responsible adults in constructive and enjoyable activities, including supervised activities with their A- and B-category friends and peers, the lower the risk of all types of chemical abuse, especially if their friends are drug and alcohol free. If the children are temperamentally difficult, the risks decrease in proportion to the level of adult supervision.

CRIME AND GANG AFFILIATION

Unsupervised Peers: The more time children spend with other children, unsupervised by responsible adults, the greater the risk for all types of criminal and gang-related behavior, especially if their associates already engage in such behavior. If the children are temperamentally difficult, the risks increase significantly.

Parents, Adults, and Supervised Peers: The more time children spend with their parents and other responsible adults in constructive and enjoyable activities, including supervised activities with their A- and B-category friends and peers, the risk of all types of criminal behavior decreases to almost zero, especially if their friends don't engage in crime. If the children are temperamentally difficult, the risks decrease in proportion to the level of adult supervision.

SCHOOL

Unsupervised Peers: The more time children spend unsupervised by responsible adults, the greater the risk for school failure, especially if they spend a lot of time with children who possess anti-school attitudes. If the children are temperamentally difficult, the risk increases.

Parents, Adults, and Supervised Peers: The more time parents spend monitoring their children and helping with their studies and homework, as needed, the lower the risk of school failure. If parents are also involved in organizing and supporting extracurricular activities at their children's schools, the risk of school failure decreases further. And if the children's friends and associates are good students, the risk of school failure decreases to a very low level. If the children are temperamentally difficult, the risks decrease in proportion to the level of adult participation in their schooling.

SEX

Unsupervised Peers: The more time children spend with other children, unsupervised by responsible adults, the greater the risk for sexual behavior, especially if their friends and peers already engage in such behavior. Even young children no more than five or six years old are at risk from sexually aggressive older children in unsupervised situations. If the children are temperamentally difficult, the risk is even greater.

Parents, Adults, and Supervised Peers: The more time children spend with their parents and other responsible adults in constructive and enjoyable activities, including supervised activities with their A- and B-category friends and peers of both sexes, the lower the risk for sexual behavior, especially if their associates aren't yet sexually active. If the children are temperamentally difficult, the risks decrease in proportion to the level of adult supervision.

WORK HABITS AND CHORES

Unsupervised Peers: The more time children spend with other children who don't clean up their messes, do their chores, or develop good work habits (at home, school, or on the job), the greater the risk of them developing the same bad habits. If the children are temperamentally-difficult, the risk factor is greater.

Parents, Adults, and Supervised Peers: The more time parents spend monitoring their children and, as needed, helping them develop good work habits and organizational skills, the lower the risk for structuring destructive work habits. This is especially true if the children's friends are also required to clean up their own mess and do specific chores. If the children are temperamentally difficult, the risks decrease in proportion to the level of adult monitoring and supervision.

Some parents and other adults, especially high school teachers and college administrators, often say, "I'm not a baby-sitter. It's not my responsibility to hold their hands. It's time they learn on their own." But the moment adults stop monitoring and supervising the children for whom they are responsible, the children's peers and associates will readily take their place. The younger the children are when they're released from responsible adult supervision and turned over to their peers, the greater the likelihood of permanent and complete life failure. Some families stop adequately supervising their children at two years old, expecting older children to supervise younger ones (*Hunter's Point: A Black Ghetto*, 1974). America has millions of five- to twelve-year-old latchkey children who spend hours each day unsupervised by responsible adults. And virtually everywhere there is a dearth of supervised daily activities and programs for the millions of thirteen- to seventeen-year-olds who are at the highest risk for death, drug use, crime, rape, molestation, gang violence, and other present-day childhood horrors. Nowhere is this more visible than in America's inner cities and in communities and neighborhoods with large numbers of overwhelmed single parents, where children kill children, children rape children, children impregnate children, and children rob children.

The key to protecting children from the real physical and social dangers currently victimizing millions of American children lies in providing the level of supervision each and every child needs. After providing a minimum safety net of supervision for all— parents always need to know what their children are doing, who they're doing it with, and where they are—the specific level of supervision each child needs above the safety net depends on his or her level of trust: the more trustworthy the child, the less direct supervision that child needs; the less trustworthy, the more direct supervision the child needs. Keep in mind that age has little to do with trust and freedom. There are many ten-year-olds who have earned more trust and deserve more freedom than their seventeen-year-old siblings.

To regain control and bring out-of-control children back into the family, it is essential that parents sever their children's bonds with negative peers and with the corrupt child-based cultures to which they belong.

Why Children Continue to Misbehave: Flawed Substitutes for Monitoring and Supervision

The only consistently dependable way to get difficult children to behave well and to habituate good behavior is through the three elements of structuring: discipline, supervision, and love. In part, because everything else allows choice or promotes inconsistency, alternative methods of improving children's behavior are doomed. What follows is a comprehensive list of the traditional, yet flawed, methods of controlling misbehaving children, and why they don't work.

PUNISHMENT

Punishment is ineffective and unreliable because it gives children a choice: they can obey the rules, or they can pay a penalty for doing as they please. Punishment also gives temperamentally difficult children many opportunities to challenge, manipulate, provoke, and control their parents and teachers.

Steve is fourteen years old, and he is close to totally irresponsible when it comes to cleaning his room. He was sitting on his bed, in the underwear he slept in, looking through car magazines as his mother came into his cluttered bedroom. Clean and dirty clothes covered much of the floor, along with magazines, dirty dishes, and trash. It was about nine o'clock on Saturday morning.

"Steven," said his mother, with a strong hint of frustration in her voice, "you've been telling me all week that you would clean this room, but it's still a mess; you haven't done anything."

"I'll do it," Steve said impatiently. "Okay?"

She paused in the doorway and turned to look at Steve. "If it isn't cleaned up by noon, you're grounded for the weekend. Okay?" she said, mimicking Steve's impatience.

"Do as you please," Steve said indifferently.

"I will," Mom said as she walked away.

Over the next couple of hours Mom checked to see if Steve was cleaning. Each time she warned him about the twelve-o'clock deadline. At noon she walked in and found that Steve, instead of picking up the mess on the bedroom floor, had added a cereal bowl, a spoon, and a juice glass to it.

"I warned you," said Mom. "Now you're grounded for the weekend."

"Like I told you," said Steve, lying on the bed, "do as you please. I really don't care."

"Fine, but your grounding includes the telephone, too."

"Big deal."

"You'll think it's a big deal when your friends call."

"Right, Mom," said Steve, smirking, as his mother walked away.

Now some will say that Steve's mother wasn't tough enough, that she should have done something that really hurt him so he would be motivated to clean his room. All right, let's really get tough on Steve, and see what happens.

"Steven," said his mother, with a strong hint of frustration in her voice, "you've been telling me all week that you would clean this room, but it's still a mess; you haven't done anything."

"I'll do it," said Steve impatiently. "Okay?"

She paused in the doorway and turned to look at Steve. "If it isn't cleaned up by noon, I'll strip your room of everything. Okay?" she said, mimicking Steve's impatience.

"Do as you please," Steve said indifferently.

"I will," Mom said as she walked away.

Over the next couple of hours Mom checked to see if Steve was cleaning. Each time she warned him about the twelve-o'clock deadline. At noon she walked in and found that Steve, instead of picking up the mess on the bedroom floor, had added a cereal bowl, a spoon, and a juice glass to it.

"I warned you," said Mom. "When your father gets home we're going to take everything out of here and put it in the garage."

"Like I told you," said Steve, getting up from the bed and walking out of the bedroom, "do as you please. I really don't care."

"Fine, but that means your TV and stereo, too," she said as she followed him into the hallway.

"Take everything you want to."

"You won't be such a smart-mouth when you're sleeping on the floor."

"Anything you say, Mom," said Steve, walking away, his room still a mess.

That evening his parents removed all the furniture from his still-messy room.

Now no doubt some people are still saying that Steve's mother still wasn't tough enough, that she should have used a belt on his bottom until he was ready to clean his room. So we will watch and see what happens when Mom puts a belt to Steve's butt.

"Steven," said his mother, with a strong hint of frustration in her voice, "you've been telling me all week that you would clean this room, but it's still a mess; you haven't done anything."

"I'll do it," said Steve impatiently. "Okay?"

She paused in the doorway and turned to look at Steve. "If it isn't cleaned up by noon, I'm going to strap your butt. Okay?" she said, mimicking Steve's impatience.

"Do as you please," Steve said indifferently.

"I will," Mom said as she walked away.

Over the next couple of hours Mom checked to see if Steve was cleaning. Each time she warned him about the twelve-o'clock deadline. At noon she walked in with a one-inch-wide leather belt in her hand and found that Steve, instead of picking up the mess on the bedroom floor, had added a cereal bowl, a spoon, and a juice glass to it.

"I warned you," said Mom. "Now turn over on your belly."

"No. I'm not going to help you hurt me."

"Then it will just land where it lands," and she swung the belt down on his thighs.

"That felt good, didn't it?" he yelled, wiggling all over the bed, trying to keep his legs out of her reach. "Enjoying yourself?"

Mom started crying in frustration. "Damn you!" she yelled, continuing to hit at his constantly moving legs.

"Hit me some more. Leave some bruises!" Steve laughed, sliding to the floor.

Mom, sobbing, flailed at any part of his body she could hit. "You little shit," she screamed. "All you had to do was clean your room."

Steve rose to his knees and scrambled into the hall as his mother knelt by the bed, sobbing.

Even severe punishment will not force some children to do as they are told. And child abuse charges could be filed in behalf of the children every time you hit them, so you put yourself in danger of having them removed from your home and placed in an institution or in a stranger's home, or having caseworkers or police officers intrude into how you discipline your children.

CREATIVE PUNISHMENT

Thirteen-year-old Josh was supposed to take out the kitchen trash every day and dump it in a bin behind his family's apartment house. On Saturdays he was to collect trash from the bathroom and bedrooms and take that out with the kitchen trash. Unfortunately, Josh apparently suffered from short-term amnesia because he seemed to never remember to take the trash out without his mother yelling and screaming at him.

One day at work, a friend of Josh's mother suggested a method that had motivated her teenage son to take out the trash on his own, and Josh's mom went home and tried it. She took the undumped trash and garbage to his room and dropped two full bags of it on the floor. But Josh ignored it. He didn't take it out, and he said nothing about it to his mother.

For the next several days the trash and garbage accumulated on his bedroom floor, taking up more and more space with each open, smelly bag. Neither Josh nor Mom said anything about it until the following Saturday when Mom, who had run out of room, started putting trash on Josh's bed. That afternoon a social worker from Children's Protective Services came to the apartment to investigate an "anonymous" complaint that children in the home were sleeping in garbage.

The social worker, who was a mother of teenage children herself, clearly understood the situation and quietly and privately told Mom she would have to find another way to get Josh to take out the trash. And after she left, Josh did take out all of the trash and put it where it belonged; but he did it under the piercing gaze of his angry mother, who was following through and monitoring the trash removal based on Josh's actual level of trust.

PUNISHMENT AT SCHOOL

Titus, in the eighth grade for the second time, walked to his desk in the back of the classroom. He was late. Everyone else was already doing an assignment written on the board while the teacher took attendance. He grabbed a pencil off of a girl's desk and threw it high in the air. It landed on a victim's head on the other side of the room.

"Titus," said his teacher, "you're not to throw anything in this class, and you know it. Your name is going down on the board. Now get busy on your assignment."

Titus shrugged his shoulders and flopped down in his seat. He picked up his book bag and looked through it for a pencil. "Hey, man," he said, reaching out and putting his hand on the desk next to his. "Got a pencil?"

"All right, Titus. You know you're to come to class prepared and that you're not to bother other students," said his teacher. "You now have earned two checks on the board. That means you owe me fifteen minutes of your lunch period."

"I didn't bother anybody," he protested, just as the boy across from him handed him a pencil. "Hey, man, did I bother you?" The boy shook his head. "See, he'll tell you. I didn't bother anybody."

"As hard as you may try, Mr. Jackson, you will not provoke me. You have just earned another check for talking back, and a trip to the assistant principal's office. And today it took you less than five minutes."

"Okay by me," Titus said, grabbing his book bag and the misconduct referral. "I didn't want to be in this fuckin' class anyway." He slammed the door as he left to face the assistant principal's punishment. Since he hadn't gone to his last three assigned detentions, he was suspended for the rest of that day and for the next two days. During that two-and-a-half-day suspension he burglarized two homes and "tagged" a dozen walls, two garages, and a minimarket. He also smoked marijuana and some rock cocaine.

Punishment, while effective some of the time with some children—those who can look ahead, see and care about consequences, and weigh them accurately—is one of the least effective means of getting temperamentally difficult children to obey rules. Punishment doesn't deter the misbehavior of those children who act on impulse and without thought, or on those who are willing to accept pain or deprivation as an acceptable trade-off for doing as they please. And many children are more than willing to be punished—as long as they can have their way. More often than not, temperamentally difficult children use their parents' punishment as a weapon of their own against their mothers and fathers. Punishment, by its very nature, is situational and inconsistent, and as a result, it creates no new habit patterns, routines, or structure for children to follow.

The Solution: It's extremely difficult to build structure by using punishment, and one can never rely on punishment to change the behavior of temperamentally difficult children. Instead, their behavior must be structured through the elements of discipline (clearly defining and stating your rules, monitoring and following through to ensure compliance, and consistency), supervision (knowing and approving of where your children are, who they are with, and what they are doing, and keeping them away from negative peers and associates), and attachment (being there with them and for them).

REWARDS

Rewards work to change behavior only when the temperamentally difficult child wants something badly enough to think about it constantly. But once he has what he wants, rewards are next to useless.

Fourteen-year-old Paul is sitting on his unmade bed, sulking, when his father comes in to talk to him. He is still angry at his mother because she yelled at him — just because he left jars of jelly and peanut butter out on the kitchen counter and jelly blobs on the living room carpet; a loaf of bread opened and drying out, a dirty knife, and a glass half full of milk on the counter; and dirty dishes in the sink.

Dad sits down next to Paul and says, "I'll make you a deal. I'll buy you that sound system we saw at Sears last Saturday if you will cooperate with your mother and clean up your messes like she wants you to."

"For how long?"

"A month, okay?"

"Buy it for me now and I will."

"No, you'll have to earn it."

"Then I won't do it. You or Mom would find some reason not to give it to me, anyway."

Like punishment, rewards give children a choice between obeying the rule and getting a reward, or doing as they please and not getting a reward. Many, many children prefer to do as they please.

The Solution: Using rewards is never a dependable way to build structure, and it rarely works. Don't depend on rewards to change the behavior of children, especially uncooperative, temperamentally difficult children. Instead, restructure their behavior through discipline, supervision, and attachment. This is not to say that children shouldn't be rewarded for good behavior, and there are many good reasons to do so. Changing their behavior just isn't one of them.

REASONING AND LECTURING

Reasoning, by itself, is almost totally ineffective in changing children's behavior, and lecturing makes children angry and frustrated.

"Honey, you're only fifteen years old. He's nineteen. That's too old for you," said Mom, sitting on Holly's bed.

"You're more than four years younger than Dad, and it hasn't hurt you two," replied Holly.

"I was twenty-six when I met your father, and we didn't get married until I was almost twenty-eight. There's a big difference between nineteen and fifteen and twenty-six and thirty-one."

"You just don't like Harold, admit it."

"Holly, he's on parole. He just got out of prison. He shot a man. He doesn't have a job. He dropped out of school. He's already fathered at least one baby. What's not to like?" Mom asked sarcastically.

"See, you're always doing that. Because he made a couple of mistakes, you won't even give him a chance."

"It's not a couple of mistakes. He's been on this path for several years now," said Mom.

"He's changed since I've met him. He even wants to go to church with us sometime."

"Do you ever read Dear Abby or Ann Landers? Their columns are full of letters from women who thought they were going to change some man. It just doesn't work that way."

"He's not like them. He's different," Holly said.

"That's what those women said, too."

"Mom, leave it alone. I love him, and nothing you can say is going to change that. If you and Dad can't accept him, that's your problem."

The part of the human brain that controls emotions and feelings has no direct connection to the part that controls logic and reasoning, and both process the information they receive independently of one another. In terms of its relative power over decision-making, logic is weak and ineffectual when compared to the enormous power of human emotion. If reason and logic were stronger than emotion, virtually none of us would be fat, and none of us would smoke or abuse alcohol or drugs. And no temperamentally difficult children would throw tantrums, say mean and hateful things, or physically hurt the people they love. And certainly none of them would grow up to rob, rape, or kill.

Using logic and reasoning to talk temperamentally difficult children out of emotionally based decisions is about as successful as trying to persuade a rock to walk. Picture a normal, slightly intoxicated fifteen-year-old boy in bed with a beautiful, sexually agressive, intoxicated twenty-year-old woman who picked him up at a party. This boy has been repeatedly warned about the dangers of having sex with strangers and the dangers of unprotected sex. But as she straddles his hips, her breasts rubbing against his face, and reaches back to put him inside her, no lecture, no force of logic, no amount of reasoning is going to cause this boy to remove his penis prematurely. His decision, right or wrong, will be based on emotion and impulse.

If he went into a convenience store with a new friend and the friend picked up a six-pack of beer, put it under his jacket, and said, "Stay between me and the clerk as we walk out," this fifteen-year-old would make, for right or wrong, another emotionally based decision. Because logic and reasoning play virtually no part in deciding whether to steal a six-pack of beer, other than possibly deciding how to outwit the store clerk, he will use none. If this fifteen-year-old is willful and impulsive, and if he wishes to be accepted by his new friend, he may join in on the theft. But if he has a patient temperament, if he is well attached to his family, and if his parents have well defined and enforced rules against stealing, just the thought of being known as a thief will overwhelm him with shame.

Rape, robbery, wife-beating, murder, gang shootings, and racial violence are by their very nature unreasonable, thoughtless acts. No amount of reasoning, logic, or lecturing can overcome bad habits or uncontrolled emotions. To see just how little reasoning and logic have to do with determining children's misbehavior, just ask your children why they misbehaved. You will almost always hear either "I don't know" or "Because I felt like it." Both answers are accurate. The children acted on impulse and emotion and probably didn't think about their misbehavior at all. If they did think about it, it was probably to figure out how they could get away with it.

To make matters worse, no one likes to be reasoned with or lectured, and when we try to reason with children we often find ourselves in arguments. And it is a rare day indeed when we find our children sincerely saying, "You're right, Dad. I haven't been responsible about taking care of my dog. I'm sorry you've had to yell at me for not keeping water in her dish, for not feeding her every day, and for not picking up after her. Now that you've explained the importance of taking care of my pet, I'll never overlook it again. Thanks for talking to me."

The Solution: Never try more than once or twice to reason with a child about continuing misbehavior. After repeatedly hearing why they should behave in a certain way, misbehaving children know your position, and they either disagree with you or don't care what you think. Instead of lecturing and reasoning with them, which frequently produces arguments, restructure their behavior through discipline, supervision, and attachment.

COMPROMISING

Dad opened the front door as he heard Leslie get out of the car in front of the house. "You were supposed to be home an hour ago," Dad said as sixteen-year-old Leslie walked into the house. "Why are you late again?"

"Dad, no one else has to be home at eleven o'clock, and it's hard to get someone to leave and bring me home early."

"What about your friend Betty? She has to be home earlier than you."

Leslie looked at her father as though he was suggesting they sit down and eat rotten meat. "She's weird. I don't hang around with her."

"You did until a couple of months ago. Is she weird because her parents make her come home early?"

"That has nothing to do with it. She's weird, that's all," she said, and then added, "Can we compromise, please? Let me stay out until midnight. I promise, if you let me stay out until midnight, I'll never be late again. Please, Dad."

Dad thought about it for a moment, decided that perhaps the eleven-o'clock curfew was unreasonable, and said, "I'll have to talk to your mother about it, but I think you'll be allowed to stay out until midnight from now on. But I'm counting on you to keep your promise."

"Oh, thank you, Daddy," she said. "You can count on me."

A week later Dad was waiting at the front door again. It was almost one o'clock when Leslie walked in the house.

"I'm glad you finally got home safely," said Dad. "But you promised me you would come home on time if I extended your curfew to midnight."

"I called and left a message on voice mail telling you I was going to get home late."

"That's not good enough. You were supposed to be home at twelve."

"I couldn't help it. No one else was leaving early. Everyone wanted to stay until the party was over."

"That's what you told me last week. But you promised if your curfew was extended you'd be home on time. You promised."

"It's not my fault. You still want me to come home too early."

The Solution: There are many good reasons why parents, at times, may compromise with a child about household rules, standards, schedules, or curfews. But never use compromise as a way to gain compliance with your rules. If you do, your children will start to believe that the best way to get you to give in and change your rules is to challenge them until you compromise. And every temperamentally difficult child knows that if parents compromise once, they'll compromise twice.

Instead of trying to get your children to behave by compromising your rules, restructure the children's behavior through discipline, supervision, and attachment.

Shape Up or Ship Out

Many smart-mouthed kids foolishly tell their parents that they are going to run away from home and away from their mean parents—that is, parents who won't let them do as they please. They say they'll go to a foster home where people will treat them fairly—that is, let them do as they please, or they'll go to Grandma's and live with someone who understands them—that is, lets them do as they please. Other children compare their parents unfavorably with those of their friends or others. Or they will complain about the quality or quantity of material goods that parents provide: "I don't like hamburger." "I don't wear clothes from K mart." "You never get anything good to drink." "This car is too old."

Unfortunately, many parents impulsively respond to their children's thoughtless provocations with suggestions that give children permission to leave home: "If you can find someone else to put up with your garbage, go ahead and leave." "Don't let the door hit you in the butt on your way out." "Hey, I'll help you pack." "Don't let us stop you." "Go ahead and find a family willing to meet your champagne tastes." Children looking for an excuse to leave home will take those statements to heart and not only leave but tell all of their friends and others that they were kicked out of their homes. On top of that, they rarely learn the hard lessons of life that parents have in mind. Instead, they successfully sponge off their friends and others, sometimes for weeks at a time. But, tragically, some do wind up on the street, where no caring parent could want a child to live for even a day.

The Solution: Never respond to children's provocations by letting them believe that they can choose to live elsewhere. (Big-mouthed twenty- or thirty-year-olds who complain that you don't do enough for them, however, can promptly be shown the door.) Instead of reacting to children's provocations, learn to deflect and sponge arguments, as described earlier.

SCARED STRAIGHT AND OTHER ONE-TIME OR OCCASIONAL STRATEGIES

Many parents with out-of-control children try to get their children into juvenile hall, jail, or prison to show them what their lives will be like in the future if they don't change their ways. More often than not they are turned away, which is just as well. The research on prison programs like those at Rahway State Prison in New Jersey, which was depicted on the *Scared Straight* television shows, demonstrate that, at best, they are ineffective. In fact, the initial research conducted on the delinquent children who went inside Rahway and were lectured with threats and dirty talk by tough, macho, physically powerful convicts indicated that they were more likely to commit new crimes than those in the control group who never went to Rahway.

There is no substitute for structure. Regardless of how tough, frightening, and emotionally charged it may be, no one-time, occasional, or short-term program can replace consistent, dependable structure. For some kids a trip to prison, jail, or juvenile hall is little more than a brief adventure. For others, the experience provides the material for outrageous stories and heroic tales to share with delinquent friends for months or years to follow.

The Solution: Never depend on a *Scared Straight* type program or any other short-term approach to change children's misbehavior.

Instead, restructure their behavior through consistent discipline, supervision, and attachment.

THERAPY

Therapy almost never dependably improves the behavior of out-of-control children. To be effective, therapy requires patients who want to change and will work together with their therapist (*A Systematic Approach to Effective Helping*, 4th edition, 1990, p. 8). Most out-of-control children are already getting their way. What, from their standpoint, do they have to gain from changing? Successful therapy also requires "motivation, commitment, and follow-through" (*The Consumer's Guide to Psychotherapy*, 1992, p. 27), something most out-of-control children have a difficult time sustaining. Finally, mandated therapy on an unwilling client is all but useless (*Consumer's Guide*, p. 27), and no clients are more unwilling to change than temperamentally difficult, out-of-control children.

Although virtually all out-of-control children need to restructure their lives, most of the mental health models used to treat difficult children are either unstructured or designed to de-structure children's daily routines. Described below are the most common therapeutic models used on out-of-control children and their parents.

Democratic Parenting Therapy: The advocates of democratic parenting are adamantly against parents imposing their values on their children. Along with Dinkmeyer and McKay, they don't want parents monitoring homework or "snupervising" children's school activities (*The Parent's Guide, STEP/Teen*). And they don't want parents telling children they must obey household rules (*Parent Effectiveness Training, P.E.T.*). Some democratic parenting counselors openly advocate that children experiment with drugs, alcohol, and sex so they can develop their own values independently of their parents (*Double Duty: Parenting Our Kids While Reparenting Ourselves*, 1990). And even though parents, or their insurance companies, may pay the therapist thousands of dollars to improve the behavior and attitudes of their difficult children, few democratic parenting professionals will candidly admit that their goal is to free misbehaving children of parental authority.

Natural and Logical Consequences: This parenting model encourages parents to stop enforcing rules and to allow the child to experience either the natural consequences that flow from a particular behavior or the logical consequences that are directly related to specific misbehavior. Above all else, parents are not to use their authority to get children to obey rules. Rudolf Dreikers, for instance, tells parents to allow bed-wetters to sleep in their own waste; to say nothing to children who steal, but instead to be their friend; to ignore children who don't do their household chores; to leave the room if your child picks his nose, telling him you're leaving because you don't like to watch him pick his nose; and "if necessary, [to] leave the house if a teenager is breaking up furniture and windows in a temper tantrum" (*Coping with Children's Misbehavior,* 1972). Natural and logical consequences don't work on uncooperative, temperamentally difficult children. They turn power and control within the family over to misbehaving children.

Contracting: This therapeutic model has therapists helping parents and children set up a contract that spells out the duties of parents and children as well as the consequences for default, just like responsible adults agreeing to the terms of a business contract. Unfortunately, the very fact that parents have sought out a counselor to help them get their children to obey household rules demonstrates that the children involved are not yet responsible. And contracting with irresponsible people of any age is self-defeating. Irresponsible kids don't follow through with their part of the contract, and parents spin their wheels administering consequences for contract defaults. No positive structure is built.

Mediating: In this model, therapists and counselors act as mediators and middlemen, negotiating household rules, tasks, and curfews between parents and children, often with no absolute value base. Both parties are usually treated as equals with parental authority either ignored or eliminated.

This approach to children's misbehavior makes positive structuring almost impossible. Worse, once kids learn they can get their way through the use of a mediator, parental authority is automatically decreased, and it becomes harder for parents to maintain control of any structure.

Behavior Modification: Behavior modification, a highly structured use of punishment and reward to change children's behavior, is frequently used by those who work with misbehaving children in institutions and schools. If it is used consistently, all but the most temperamentally difficult children will follow the institution's rules most of the time. Unfortunately, there is rarely any carryover when the children go home. When children simply concentrate on getting rewards and avoiding punishment, rather than on rules or tasks, they fail to habituate new behavior patterns. Behavior modification requires more time and energy than most parents can provide and is even less effective at home than in an institutional setting.

Mental health therapy does many things that are good, but changing the behavior of difficult, incorrigible, delinquent, and criminal children is not one of them. In fact, until such children's behavior has been restructured, it is difficult for therapists to diagnose or treat children's mental health problems.

The Solution: Don't rely on unstructured mental health therapy to change your children's misbehavior. Instead, restructure the children's behavior through consistent discipline, supervision, and attachment. If you feel you need professional support and direction to regain control of your misbehaving children, or if there are mental health problems to be overcome in addition to behavior problems, find a therapist or counselor who supports the parents' right to set and enforce rules for their children.

EDUCATION

Many American educators, liberal therapists, and children's rights activists, seeing the enormous problem of children's drug and alcohol abuse, sexually transmitted diseases, and pregnancies, have proposed numerous "least-restrictive" and nonauthoritative methods of solving these problems. The most common one is education. Unfortunately for the parents and children, however, emotionally generated behavior cannot be changed by education. After spending billions of dollars to educate children about drugs, America now has the best-educated, most knowledgeable drug users in the world. And soon America will have the best-educated, most knowledgeable group of sexually active HIV-infected young people in the world. The decision to use or not to use a condom almost never has an academic or educational basis. Most people who refuse to use condoms know how and why to use them. For a variety of feelings, however, they choose not to do so.

If education could change emotionally based behavior, no one would steal, rape, batter, assault, or rob others: "Judge, no one ever told me. If only my schools had let me know that I shouldn't fuck strange women at knifepoint, I never would have done it. . . . What? Is that right? Hey, I'm sorry. I didn't know the word 'fuck' was offensive to some people. Well, what can I say? My school never taught me that, either. But now that I've learned that these things are bad, I'll never do them again."

Again, nothing can replace the three elements within the ethological milieu that structure people's behavior: consistent discipline, supervision, and attachment. No amount of education will stop drug use, drunkenness, school failure, sex, violence, and crime, because people rarely use their intellect to decide to misbehave, only their emotions.

7

HOW TO REGAIN CONTROL OF OUT-OF-CONTROL CHILDREN

If parents don't consistently discipline their out-of-control children, who will?

If parents don't consistently supervise their out-of-control children, who will?

If parents don't consistently reach out to their out-of-control children with love, who else can?

The First Steps in Gaining Control

Children who have learned that violence is an effective means of getting their way will use violence until they are stopped. Chronic runaways who learn that they don't have to obey any household rules if they aren't at home will continue to run away until they are stopped. Children who are emotionally attached to powerful peer cliques and subcultures like street gangs, skinheads, punks, heavy metalers, alternative kids, and graffiti taggers draw enormous amounts of antiparent, antiauthority support from their peers. Until they are prevented from having any contact with these people, children will fight every parental attempt at regaining control. Of all of the things that parents must do to regain control, it is most important and most difficult to stop the violence, prevent the running away, and end the peer-group influence.

If your teenage children are violent, aggressive, and quick to lose their temper, if they hit or physically manhandle you to get their way, if they are chronic runaways, or if they are deeply involved in gangs or delinquent and incorrigible subcultures, please consider sending them to a well-structured, well-supervised wilderness program or residential treatment center, or participating in a Back in Control Parenting Workshop as a first step in regaining control.

Some types of misbehavior are obviously worse than others. If your children are involved in drugs, alcohol abuse, running away, crime, or gang activity, or if they are associating with destructive people, work on those problems before attempting to get them to clean their rooms, take out the trash, do their homework, or perform any other tasks or chores. If a sixteen-year-old girl's primary problem is cutting school to hang out with her drug-using friends, don't try to get her to clean her room or do her homework at this time. That will come later. Instead, work on keeping her in class, removing her from her negative peers, and providing day-to-day supervision based on her level of trust. In two or three weeks, after you have initially regained control, you may begin to work on household tasks and homework.

Also, before you work on anything, reread Chapter 5, "Provocation and Manipulation," and practice handling your children's attempts to overcome, dismantle, or avoid your discipline and supervision.

Controlling Alcohol, Drugs, Tobacco, and Crime

The most effective way to control alcohol, drugs, tobacco, and participation in crime is through clearly defined rules and consistent and dependable supervision. Set out below are some sample rules regarding alcohol, drugs, tobacco, and crime. Choose the ones that best meet your standards and values and use them as they are or revise them to meet your children's specific needs. Please note that these rules are mandatory and clearly tell children to do or not do something.

SAMPLE RULES

(Some of these rules are inconsistent with one another. Please select those that are compatible with your values and goals.)

- Never drink alcohol.
- Never drink alcohol until you are of legal age, and even then never drink to get high.
- Never associate with people who drink alcohol until you are of legal age.
- With Mom or Dad's permission, you may have a glass of beer or wine with a meal, but until you are of legal age, never drink alcohol with your friends or anyone else, and never drink to get drunk.
- Call Mom or Dad, call a friend, or call a cab, but never drink and drive, and never ride with a driver who's under the influence of alcohol.
- Never use or possess any illegal drugs, and never associate with those who do.
- Never use or possess tobacco of any kind until you are an adult, and never use tobacco in my presence or in this house.
- Don't associate with friends and peers who use tobacco.
- Never sell, transport, hold, or have anything to do with the sale of illegal drugs, and never associate with anyone who does.
- Never steal anything.
- Never take anything that doesn't belong to you without the owner's permission.
- Never buy or hold stolen goods.
- Never associate with people who steal or are involved in other crimes. If anyone you are with attempts to steal or commit another crime, do your best to stop the person, or leave immediately and contact Mom or Dad. This is an extremely serious issue. Simply being with someone who is committing a crime is enough in most states to be charged with the same crime unless one takes obvious action to prevent it, or leaves the scene before the crime starts.

PREVENTING SUBSTANCE ABUSE AND CRIME

Few children start drinking, using drugs, smoking tobacco, or stealing (the most common crime) on their own or because of parental encouragement. Virtually all teenage and preteen drinking, drug use, smoking, and crime start with children's friends and associates and with unsupervised freedom. Children's chemical abuse and crime start and continue only when adult supervision falls short, and adults, especially parents, don't know where their children are, who they are with, or what they are doing. Furthermore, there is a direct relationship between unsupervised freedom and the risk of all dangerous behaviors. The more freedom from supervision children have and the longer they have it, the greater the risk.

To reduce the risk of your children ever using alcohol, drugs, or tobacco or being engaged in crime, it is crucial that you know where your children are, who they are with, and what they are doing. Also, you need to establish and enforce rules against your children being in other people's homes when the parents are not home. Except under your direct supervision, don't let your children associate with children you don't know well and whose parents you don't know well. Also, don't let your kids hang out with their friends except at your home or in the home of a neighbor or friend whom you trust implicitly and who can and will supervise a houseful of teenagers. In fact, don't let your children hang out anywhere unsupervised at any time. Don't let them cruise the streets and boulevards or hang out at the mall or at a convenience store.

Now, reading this you may have a fit, because kids have always hung out. But today's parents have to decide how much risk they are willing to subject their children to. Allowing them the freedom to cruise or hang out dramatically increases their risk for virtually every behavior problem. The fact that other kids do it, and that kids have been doing it for generations, doesn't make it safe or acceptable, especially since today's American teenagers and preteens lead the world in every type of destructive, dangerous behavior.

Don't let your children go to parties unless you have personally talked to the people hosting the party. Make sure that no alcohol or drugs will be permitted, that the supervision is adequate (at least one adult for every eight to ten kids and always an adult monitoring the door), and that most of the kids attending the party know one another.

Never let your children go to open parties where you have no way of knowing who will be in attendance. Also, don't let them go to teenage nightclubs. Even the best clubs have no way of excluding, or even recognizing, alcohol or drug abusers and young criminals who can have a powerful influence on your children. In the late 1980s the Back in Control Centers in Southern California worked with more than a dozen families each fall whose children had started behaving dangerously after emotionally bonding with strangers they met night after night during the summer at the well-supervised teenage nightclubs (since closed) at Disneyland and Knott's Berry Farm. The level of supervision provided at Knott's Berry Farm, and especially at Disneyland, could not be much better. No alcohol, drugs, or weapons are allowed. Neither is sex. And any boy who thinks it's fun to feel up unsuspecting girls on the crowded dance floor is quickly escorted out the front gate, or he winds up talking to a police officer. But there is no way any amusement park or other public place can protect your children from bonding with negative peers. Fortunately, you can.

Of all the things parents can do to protect their children from alcohol, drugs, tobacco, and crime, keeping them busy and occupied with school, church, community, and family activities is the best. The more time children spend with responsible, trustworthy friends in positive, esteem-building activities, the less likely they will be to use alcohol, drugs, or tobacco or to commit crimes. But responsible, trustworthy children can also go to public activities, including amusement parks, skating rinks, bowling alleys, and movies as long as each place is reasonably well supervised by responsible adults and periodically monitored by parents. Kids who spend much of their time just hanging around and not actually doing anything are at highest risk for emotionally bonding to negative peers.

STOPPING CHEMICAL ABUSE AND CRIME

To regain control and stop children's alcohol, drug, or tobacco use or their participation in crime, parents must provide whatever level of monitoring and supervision their children need. And children involved at one level or another with various forms of chemical use or crime, including drug dealing, obviously need a high level of adult monitoring and supervision. Because their behavior has destroyed any trust they may have earned, seriously misbehaving children have lost the right to privacy. Their rooms and belongings should be checked regularly. Above all else, though, they need to be brought back into an adult structured and supervised world, away from the ethological milieu of their friends and associates.

They need to be in class during the school day, involved in after-school activities when school is over, and home for the evening when their after-school activities are over. On weekends they need to be with parents or other responsible adults who will provide a high degree of eyes-on supervision.

Untrustworthy children can go to movies, roller-skating, or bowling. They can go swimming, ice-skating, or bicycling. They can do almost anything they want to do, as long as they are directly supervised by responsible adults. They can even have friends over, but not those friends who commit crimes or use alcohol, drugs, or tobacco or who, because they have too much unsupervised freedom, are at risk for such behavior.

Going places and doing things will obviously depend on Mom or Dad's ability and willingness to go out of their way. Although parents are under no obligation to meet their child's every whim and desire, the more adult-directed and supervised activities children participate in, the better they will generally behave.

If you wish to significantly reduce the likelihood of your children returning to their old ways, don't allow them to have any contact with friends who have a recent history of alcohol, drug, or tobacco use or criminal behavior, even in your presence in your own home, on the telephone, or through notes or third-party contacts.

If they are still attending the same school and the same classes, ask their teachers to separate them. If they continue to meet each other at lunch, either change schools or arrange for your child to have lunch with an adult at school—a favorite teacher, the librarian, the custodian, the campus supervisor, or a counselor, for example.

As children follow the rules of their homes and earn trust, parents may appropriately reduce the level of direct eyes-on supervision they receive. But earning trust is a slow process, and one of the worst mistakes parents can make is to give children too much freedom too soon. Even the best-behaved, most trustworthy children need occasional monitoring, and parents always need to know where their children are, who they are with, and what they are doing.

Parents, by limiting the amount of unsupervised freedom they allow their children to have, determine the risk level for children's alcohol, drug, and tobacco use, and crime. By consistently using the methods described above, parents can prevent even difficult children from using alcohol, drugs, or tobacco or becoming criminals. But please keep three things in mind:

- If you don't clearly define and state your rules, your children and their friends will develop their own rules.
- If you don't follow through and enforce your rules, your children and their friends won't do it for you.
- If you don't consistently enforce your rules, your children won't consistently obey them.

Chores

Do not try to get your children to do their chores if they are using drugs and alcohol, running away, or associating with negative peers. Concentrate first on these more serious problems, because as long as your children are getting emotional support from negative peers, you will find yourself in stupid battles over the trash or over dirty bedrooms. To regain control over out-of-control children, it is imperative that you start by cutting them off from the ethological milieu that supports their continued misbehavior. Only after they have been removed from the comfort and support of their negative peers should you start to train your children to do their household chores.

Most children, even comparatively cooperative children, won't do their household chores, won't do them well, or won't do them on their own unless they are consistently trained to do so. Temperamentally difficult children are likely to do even less. In fact, getting children to do household chores is a demanding, frustrating, never-ending struggle for both parents and children. The tasks are often not clearly defined, and so the follow-through is frequently ineffective, counterproductive, and almost certainly inconsistent. Worse, children then build inconsistent and sometimes chaotic experience on their behavioral templates to be used every time their parents tell them to clean up the kitchen, empty the trash, or pick after the dog. Well, it's time for that to stop.

Set out below are some sample rules and job descriptions. Choose the ones that best meet your family's standards and values, and use them as they are or revise them to meet your children's specific needs. All of them include time schedules. Putting your children's household chores on a consistently enforced schedule will, along with deflecting and sponging arguments, do more to restore peace and harmony to your home than anything else you do. Please note that all of these rules tell children to do or not to do something. They don't allow room for choice. They must be followed as stated.

SAMPLE RULES

(Select those that are compatible with your goals.)

- Clean your room now and every Saturday morning as soon as you get up and no later than 9:00 A.M. Always use the job description for cleaning bedrooms.
- Take out the trash now. Put it in the cans next to the garage. Put a new liner in the can. Then put the can back where it belongs. Do this every day from now on as soon as you get home from school.
- Put all of your dirty clothes in the hamper. Do this every day as soon as you take them off. Never put clean or unworn clothes in the hamper.
- Clean the bathroom, according to the bathroom job description, every time you take a shower or bath from now on.

SAMPLE JOB DESCRIPTIONS

- Neatly make your bed every morning as soon as you get up. Secure the bottom sheet on the mattress, and pull up the top sheet, blankets, and bedspread, keeping the sides even, and smoothing all of the wrinkles out. Neatly place your pillows at the head of the bed under the bedspread.

- Every Monday and Wednesday take all of your dirty clothes and towels to the laundry room.
- Neatly hang up or fold all of your clean clothing every day. Place all of your shirts on hangers. Button the top button on every shirt, and hang all the shirts together, facing the same direction. Hang your pants on hangers, pant-leg seams matched. Hang all of your pants together. Fold your underwear neatly. Put your undershirts and underpants in the top drawer. Put your rolled-up socks in the second drawer. Put your neatly folded T-shirts in the third drawer. Put your shorts and swimsuits in the fourth drawer.
- Place all of your shoes, paired together on the closet floor, facing out, every day.
- Put all of your trash in the trash can each day.
- Put everything else away neatly where it belongs every day.
- Clean your bedroom every Saturday, as soon as you finish breakfast and no later than 10:00 A.M.
- Strip your bed and take the sheets and pillowcases to the washroom every Saturday, along with all of your dirty clothes and towels.
- Make up your bed with clean linen every Saturday morning. Put the fitted bottom sheet firmly and evenly on the mattress. Place the top sheet and blankets over the bottom sheet, making sure they are straight and even. Tuck the top sheet and blankets under the foot of the mattress, then along the sides until all the wrinkles are gone. Place the bedspread over the blankets, keeping the sides straight and even. Smooth out all of the wrinkles. Place pillowcases on the pillows, and put the pillows at the top of the bed under the bedspread.
- Using a dustcloth treated with an antidust spray, dust every surface in your bedroom, moving and dusting everything on those surfaces. When you are done, put the dustcloth in the clothes hamper and the antidust spray back under the kitchen sink.
- Get the vacuum cleaner from the hall closet and take it to your room. Check the bag to make sure that the dirt in bag is not above the "full" line. If it is, replace the bag according to the directions printed on the side of the bag. Then vacuum your bedroom floor, including under your bed, until everything on the floor, except the carpet and furniture, is vacuumed up. If the

vacuum won't pick everything up, use your hands. If you can't get it up, come and get Mom or Dad. When you are done, return the vacuum to the hall closet.

- Put everything back in its proper place.
- When you are done, ask Mom or Dad to check your room.
- Every time you finish taking a shower, use the sponge from the bathroom cupboard to wipe down the counter and sink until you have removed all toothpaste remains, loose hair, and soap scum. Pick up all of the dirty towels, washcloths, and clothes and put them in the laundry room.
- As soon as you finish cleaning your bedroom on Saturday morning, clean the bathroom. Go to the cabinet beneath the kitchen sink and get cleanser, glass-cleaner, toilet-bowl cleaner, and tub-and-tile cleaner. Get the bucket and pine cleaner. Also get several rags. Take it all to the bathroom.
- Take the bathroom throw rugs, towels, and washcloths to the laundry room.
- Wash the walls of the shower stall with tub-and-tile cleaner according to the directions on the can until the entire stall, including the glass door, is completely clean.
- Put three shakes of cleaner on a wet sponge and clean the bathroom sink until it is completely clean. Then thoroughly rinse all of the cleanser film off the sink.
- Squirt the toilet-bowl cleaner into the toilet bowl, including underneath the upper edge, according to the directions on the container. Using the toilet brush, brush out the toilet bowl until it is completely clean. Put two shakes of cleanser on a damp rag and completely clean the tank and its lid, the toilet-bowl rim, the top and bottom of the toilet seat, and the outside of the bowl, including the elements that connect the toilet to the floor. Then, with a clean damp rag, wipe off all of the cleanser film.
- Fill the bucket with hot water and add pine cleaner according to the directions on the bottle. Soak a medium-sized clean rag in the bucket of hot water and pine cleaner, wring it out, and wash the bathroom floor until it is completely clean, rinsing and wringing out the rag as necessary.
- Squirt five shots of window cleaner on the mirror, and using a clean dry cloth, rub the mirror until it is completely clean. Also spray the chrome fixtures in the shower and sink with window cleaner and wipe them down until they shine.

- When you are done, put the rags in the laundry room and return the toilet brush to its container by the toilet. Put everything else neatly into the cabinet under the kitchen sink.
- Come and get Mom or Dad to check the bathroom when you are done.

MONITORING AND FOLLOW-THROUGH

For your own mental health, it is important that you regard the process of getting your children to do their chores as nothing more than training, during which parents need to monitor household jobs according to how well their children work independently. Specifically, children who aren't yet doing their jobs well, or on a schedule, need an adult with them while they are working. But the better they do their chores on their own, the less closely parents need to monitor their performance. Think about it. From your experience, if your children aren't good about doing their chores, what almost always happens when you don't monitor them? Most kids are just as consistent about doing their chores as parents are about monitoring. And if you want your children to do their chores well on their own, then monitor them according to the level of trust they have earned.

If your children won't do their chores properly without your presence, plan on monitoring the total job at least the first five or six times. On a day when you see they are doing their work with momentum, leave for three or four minutes. If they continue to work well while you are gone, leave for five or six minutes the next day. If that is successful, you can get them started, check on them once or twice during the job, and check when it's over. Then, when you get to the point where you need to monitor children's chores only occasionally, you can get them started, and then check the job when it is done.

This whole process, from totally undependable to reasonably dependable, normally takes only three to four weeks maximum for daily chores, and two to three months for weekly chores. The longer the children follow these new routines, the stronger their behavioral templates will become, and the more organized and independent they will be. However, if during the first few weeks of minimal monitoring something interrupts the children's daily routines—illness, for example, or vacation or school activities—you may need to closely monitor chore schedules for a few days to restore their newly acquired habit patterns.

CONSISTENCY

If you are consistent in enforcing chore schedules, your children will consistently follow those schedules. If you don't have a schedule, you are training your children to put off doing their chores until you remind them. And if you typically remind them three or more times before you follow through, you are training your children to believe that they don't have to obey you at least two-thirds of the time. Please keep three facts in mind:

- If you don't clearly set out your children's household chores with written job descriptions, your children aren't likely to do so on their own.
- If you don't follow through and monitor your children's chores on a schedule, your children won't do it for you.
- If you aren't consistent about enforcing your rules on a schedule, your children won't follow a routine and will continue to wait for you to tell them what to do.

Gangs, Delinquent Subcultures, and Criminal Peer Cliques

Getting kids out of gangs and other delinquent and incorrigible cliques requires consistent and dependable supervision, but you must first clarify and define the rules your children are to follow. Set out below are typical sample rules. Choose the ones that best meet your family's standards and values. Use as they are, or revise them to meet your children's specific needs. Please note that all of these rules tell children to do or not do something. They are mandatory and do not allow room for choice.

SAMPLE RULES

(Please select those rules that are compatible with your values and goals.)

- Never join a gang or become part of a delinquent clique of skinheads, taggers, punks, or heavy metalers, and never associate with anyone who does.
- Never have anything to do with gangs or gang members or delinquent cliques and subcultures of skinheads, heavy metalers, punks, or taggers in any way.
- Never wear clothing, jewelry, shoes, or hairstyles that are associated with gangs, delinquent cliques, or negative subcultures of skinheads, heavy metalers, punks, or taggers, and never associate with those that do.

SUPERVISION

Prevention: Few children become gangsters, heavy metalers, skinheads, taggers, or punks on their own or because of parental encouragement. Virtually all gang and delinquent clique and subculture activities start when kids become emotionally attached to friends, peers, and associates who are already a part of the gang or clique and, in some cases, when children become emotionally attached to musicians and bands who seem to be a part of a specific delinquent subculture. The longer children associate with those to whom they are emotionally attached, the more they habituate their behavior patterns, attitudes, values, and even clothing styles. Ironically, parents often worsen the situation by paying for the clothes, jewelry, and hairstyles that distinguish members of gangs and incorrigible cliques from everyone else. And more often than not, parents have no idea that they are helping their children reinforce their identity as gangsters, heavy metalers, punks, skinheads, or taggers.

The risk of children becoming part of a delinquent gang, clique, or subculture is directly related to the amount of unsupervised freedom they are given. The more freedom they have to associate with gangsters, delinquents, and wanna-bes (C-category associates), the greater the risk that the children will bond with the group or with individuals in the group. And the more freedom they have to wear the clothes, jewelry, and hairstyles of the gang, clique, or subculture, the more likely they will emotionally bond to the group and its values and styles of behavior.

To prevent children from becoming members of delinquent gangs, cliques, or subcultures, always know and approve of where your children are, who they are with, and what they are doing. Establish and enforce rules against your children being in other people's homes when the parents are not present. Except under your direct supervision, don't let your children associate with children you don't know well (B-category associates) and whose parents you don't know well. And don't let your children associate with kids you believe to be associated with delinquent gangs, cliques, or subcultures (C-category associates), even if you are supervising them.

Also, don't let your kids hang out with their friends, except at your home or in the home of a neighbor or friend whom you trust implicitly and who can supervise a houseful of teenagers. Hanging out, away from direct adult supervision, is essential for the formation of a gang or delinquent clique, so don't let your children hang out unsupervised at any time. Don't let them cruise the streets or hang out at the mall or at a convenience store.

Of all the things parents can do to protect their children from gangs and other negative peer influences, keeping them busy and occupied with school, church, community, and family activities is the best. The more time children spend with responsible, trustworthy friends (A-category associates) in constructive activities, the less likely they will be to join a gang or attach themselves to delinquent cliques or subcultures.

GETTING KIDS OUT OF DELINQUENT GANGS, CLIQUES, AND SUBCULTURES

To get kids out of delinquent gangs, cliques, and subcultures, parents must provide the maximum level of monitoring and supervision while bringing them back into an adult-structured and -supervised world, away from their negative friends and associates. All of the clothing, jewelry, and other items associated with their specific gang, clique, or subculture should be disposed of. Hairstyles should be returned to normal, and after everything else is under control a dermatologist should be consulted about the removal of any inappropriate tattoos. Get rid of your children's tapes and CDs of music supporting their negative peer cultures. Also, if your children are gangsters, go through their rooms and remove all weapons (guns, knives, brass knuckles) and drug paraphernalia. If they are taggers, remove all spray paint, markers, and other supplies and equipment used for their graffiti assaults on the neighborhood. If they are skinheads, get rid of their Nazi flags, posters, and war souvenirs as well as their collection of U.S. military pins, badges, and insignia. In other words, get rid of absolutely everything associated with a particular gang, clique, or subculture.

Children need to be in school during the school day, involved in after-school activities when school is over, and home for the evening when their after-school activities are over. On weekends they need to be with parents or other responsible adults who will provide a high degree of eyes-on supervision.

Children who have earned little or no trust can still go to the movies, roller-skating, or bowling; they can go swimming, ice-skating, or bicycling; they can do almost anything they want to do, as long as they are directly supervised by responsible adults. They can even have friends over, but not those who were or are gangsters, skinheads, heavy metalers, punks, taggers, or kids with too much freedom.

If you wish to significantly reduce the likelihood of your children returning to their old ways, don't allow them to have any contact with their old C-category friends, even in your presence in your own home, on the telephone, through notes, or by way of third-party contacts.

If they are still attending the same school and they share classes, ask their teachers to separate them from their former friends in the classroom. If they continue to meet each other at lunch, either change schools or arrange for your child to eat lunch with an adult at school—a favorite teacher, for example, or the librarian, the custodian, the campus supervisor, or a counselor.

CONSISTENCY

Consistent adult supervision is the most important element in removing children, even difficult children, from delinquent and criminal peer groups. There is a direct relationship between the amount of freedom children receive and their risk for joining delinquent gangs, cliques, and subcultures. The greater the amount of freedom the greater the risk. And ask yourself these questions:

- If you don't consistently supervise your children's activities, who will?

- If you don't protect your children from the negative influences in their lives, who will?

Running Away

If your children have not yet run away from home, they are not likely to do so—unless they start associating with children who run away. Most children run away from home not because they have been molested, neglected, or abused but because they have made a new friend or entered a peer clique that supports running away from home. Worse yet, if runaway children stay away from home for any length of time, they may be under the influence of negative peers for close to twenty-four hours a day for days or weeks at a time. And there is no faster way to change children's behavior, attitudes, values, and beliefs, than to put them in an ethological milieu constructed by negative peers for days, weeks, or months at a time. The more time they spend on the run, away from caring, responsible adults, the stronger their newly built destructive behavioral templates become, and the more likely it is that those templates will dictate their future behavior.

In some communities, government programs or private social service agencies provide food, shelter, clothing, and even dances and parties for runaway children on the streets, encouraging them to stay on the run, out of school, and away from home. Although these agencies and programs sometimes go through the motions of reuniting runaway children with their families, they often become focal points and support centers for new runaways. They also prop open the doors to the ethological milieu created and continued by street kids. It is vital, then, that parents find their runaway children and bring them home as soon as possible. Never, never wait until "they have learned their lesson," because they may not learn the lessons you desire.

Set out below are some sample rules. Choose the ones that best meet your family's standards and values. Use as they are, or revise them to meet your children's specific needs. Please note that all of these rules tell children to do or not do something. They are mandatory and don't allow room for choice.

SAMPLE RULES

(Select those that are compatible with your values and goals.)

- Never leave home without permission or without letting Mom or Dad know where you're going to be.
- Never run away from home again.
- Never stay away from home without Mom or Dad's permission.

Prevention

The best way to prevent your children from running away is to prevent them from associating with poorly supervised friends and other negative peers, especially those with a history of running away or not coming home at night (C-category associates). Also, don't let them go to unsupervised parties or teenage nightclubs. Don't let them cruise or hang out. In other words, don't let them go to places that attract large numbers of C-category kids. If you follow this advice, the likelihood that your children will run away is next to zero.

Stopping runaway children from leaving home is one of the most difficult jobs parents may ever face. But if they don't do it, they place their children at the highest possible risk for every childhood danger.

FINDING A RUNAWAY CHILD

Most kids who run away stay with friends and associates in their own communities. However, if your children have been placed in psychiatric hospitals or chemical dependency programs that draw clients from a large metropolitan area, or if they go to teenage nightclubs that attract kids in from a large area, they could be anywhere in that metro area. Or if you have recently moved, they may be with someone in their old community. Obviously, if they are close by, where a lot of people know them, they are generally easy to find. But even if they are many miles away, parents can usually find them.

If your child runs away, report the missing child to the police as soon as possible. Most police agencies won't actually look for runaway children, but if the children are stopped by a patrol officer who checks the computer for the names of runaways, they can be taken into temporary custody and returned home.

After reporting runaway children as missing, make up a list of all the kids who could possibly know where they are or who they may be with, and contact all of them and their parents. In a notebook write down everything you are told that could possibly lead you to your runaway child, including the names, nicknames, locations, schools, and hangouts of new friends and associates. Write down when and where your missing children were last seen.

If your child has a best friend or a special boyfriend or girlfriend and you know where he or she lives, or if you get information that your missing child may be at a specific location or hangout, borrow or rent a car and stake out the location. Park down the street or around the corner where you will not be conspicuous, at a time when your child is most likely to be coming or going. You might also stake out the home, school, or workplace of the missing child's best friend and allow that person to lead you to your child.

If your missing child hangs out at a mall, a fast-food restaurant, or a convenience store, prepare flyers displaying the child's picture and your telephone number and hand them out to mall security officers and restaurant and store managers. Ask them to keep an eye out and to call you immediately if they see your child.

If you find your missing child and you believe he or she will resist going home with you, or if you believe there may be violence, ask the police to send an officer to help keep the peace. In many locations the police, as a matter of policy, will not help you pick up a runaway, but they almost always respond to calls about potential violence. So when you ask the police to help you pick up a resistant, possibly violent child, be sure to explain that you want them there to "protect the peace." Be warned, however, that in some states runaway children have been given the "right" to go to a government-sponsored shelter rather than go home with their parents. If you live in such a state, you may want to think twice before calling on the police for assistance, and instead retrieve your potentially violent runaway children with the assistance of a professional pickup service. Local residential chemical dependency programs or psychiatric hospitals should be able to give you the names and telephone numbers of these services.

If your children have a history of sneaking out of their bedroom windows and running away, secure the bedroom windows so they can't be opened. If your children run out the front door the moment you turn your back, place a double-key dead-bolt lock on the front door. If they leave your home through other doors or windows, or will go out any opening they can find, secure the house as necessary. You may want to place an inexpensive door alarm on the runaway child's bedroom door, or a motion-sensor alarm in the hallway if they are likely to sneak out in the middle of the night.

Whenever you secure any part of your house, be sure to install smoke detectors. Also set up fire escape routes and practice using them so that no one will be in danger during an emergency.

CONSISTENCY

To stop children from running away from home consistently do everything you can to convince them that running away is not one of their choices. Track them down and bring them home every time they run away. Make sure they can't leave the house without permission. And don't let them associate with negative peers (C-category associates). Please keep these questions in mind:

- If you don't protect your children from the negative influences of uncooperative, temperamentally difficult children, who will?
- If you don't consistently stop your runaway children from taking off, who will?

School Problems

If your children are using drugs or alcohol, running away, or associating with negative peers, do not immediately try to get them to do their homework. Wait until you have removed them from the anti-school, anti-parent support they receive from their negative peers.

Well-supervised, moderately disciplined schools can help even uncooperative, temperamentally difficult children achieve academic success and do well with the rest of their lives. Poorly supervised, poorly disciplined schools can destroy even well-behaved, cooperative children. Most schools dealing with sixth through twelfth graders, especially high schools, are poorly structured, especially for temperamentally difficult children. Many high schools don't promptly notify parents of class-cutting or truancies. Many schools that use computer-generated calling machines to notify parents of missed classes don't have a human follow-up in case the truant intercepts the call. Many schools encourage the development of gangs and other delinquent cliques by not enforcing a strict dress code. Many teachers don't notify parents until the end of the quarter or semester that their children haven't been turning in classwork or homework or haven't been passing tests. And many teachers as a matter of policy use a freedom-to-fail approach with students and don't bother to ask about missed classwork and homework. This means that parents have to make up for bad schools by doing the work that schools should be doing.

Set out below are typical sample rules related to schools. Choose the ones that best meet your children's needs. Use them as they are, or revise them as appropriate. Please note that all of these rules are mandatory and tell children specifically to do or not do something.

Sample Rules

(Select those that are compatible with your values and goals.)

- Never be truant from school.
- Go to school and attend every class, on time, until you graduate.
- Never leave school without Mom or Dad's permission.
- Do all of your classroom assignments to the best of your ability, and always turn them in on time.
- Do all of your homework at the kitchen table every afternoon as soon as you get in from school. Always turn it in when it's due.
- In addition to your homework, study every evening as soon as you are finished with your homework. Follow the methods set out in the "how to study" guide we bought at the bookstore.

- Never talk back to any of your teachers. If you have a problem with a teacher, talk to Mom or Dad about it, and if necessary we'll talk to the teacher or principal.
- Unless you have to protect yourself from violence, never fight at school. If someone is bothering you, tell Mom or Dad, and together, we'll solve the problem.
- Never take a weapon of any kind to school, and never possess any kind of weapon at school. Never help anyone else bring a weapon to school.
- Never vandalize your school.

MONITORING AND FOLLOW-THROUGH

If your children's schools don't promptly notify you of missed homework and classwork, poor achievement, class-cutting, or day-long truancy, buy a daily assignment book or a student's daily planner. Have your children write down all of their homework assignments, test results and other grades, and, if appropriate, how they behaved and performed in class that day. Go to all of the teachers where there appear to be problems and firmly but nicely ask them to verify with a signature the truthfulness and accuracy of what your children have written in their assignment books or planners. At the same time ask for a signature sample that you can use, if necessary, at home. If at any time you stop seeing your children doing homework or studying, assume there is a problem and speak to the teacher immediately.

If your children don't bring their assignment books or daily planners home with them, if they bring them home but there are no signatures, if the signature looks as if a ninth grader wrote it, or if anything else suspicious happens, take your children, along with their assignment books or planners, to school the following morning. Get there about thirty minutes before school starts and take your child from teacher to teacher to find out what the problem is. Do this whenever your children don't fill out their assignment books or daily planners as directed, or anytime your intuition tells you there is a problem.

If some teachers won't cooperate with you, talk to the principal. If you don't get cooperation there, go to the superintendent's office. If you still aren't getting the cooperation you need, go to the board of education. At this point you might also call the local newspaper or television news bureau and ask them to send someone to the next school board meeting. Parents who are trying to do their best for difficult children and who are not getting even minimum levels of cooperation from the school can create a powerful public image as they fight the school bureaucracy in behalf of their children. Or you can do it the easy way: put your child in a different school. Even in the same school district, one often finds significant quality differences between schools. Or, if you can afford it, consider private education.

After letting your children know in advance what you will do if they cut school again, walk them from class to class the next day. You will probably have to do this only once to convince them that you mean what you say. If you can't arrange to walk them from class to class, perhaps another family member can do so. Interestingly, the most powerful person on a child's campus, if it becomes necessary to walk the student from class to class, is Grandma. The kids might think up some reason for Mom or Dad being on campus with them, but it would be really hard to explain away Grandma's presence.

Please note that consistency is vital in controlling truancy. Some children, especially uncooperative, temperamentally difficult children, will constantly test the limits if you won't "help" them get to school every day. But the all-time record of our Back in Control parents actually having to walk truant children from class to class in reasonably well supervised schools is three days, and that record has held firm for over fifteen years. If your children go to school where little actual effort is put into getting kids to class, however, it is virtually impossible to stop truancy by yourself. Do everything you can either to change school policies that allow or promote truancy or to get your children out of that school. In some instances, if a parent is home during the day to monitor and supervise, you may want to consider home schooling through a university's accredited high school correspondence course.

If your children continually misbehave at school, go with them one time to observe the situations in which the problem occurs. If the misbehavior is in the classroom, observe the classroom dynamics. If it's outside on the playground, observe your children's behavior from the playground. In many instances you will find that the problem rests with an incompetent or poorly trained teacher who does not know how to maintain order. If so, you will probably want to press the school administration to remove your children from that class and, unfortunately, sometimes from several classes. If, however, from your observation, it is clear to you that despite the teacher's best efforts, it's your children who are the problem, the next time you get a report of serious misbehavior come and sit next to them in class and direct their behavior. Once will probably be enough if the teacher has good control over the rest of the class.

Misbehavior often occurs on school playgrounds when temperamentally difficult children are placed in unstructured situations with little supervision. Inevitably there are problems. The solution here is to either convince the school to have structured playtime for the younger children or to place more adults out on the playground to supervise at lunch or recess. On junior high and high school campuses where kids fight, set trash-can fires, grab girls' breasts or bottoms, smoke, use drugs, and extort money, the school needs to put more adults out to supervise—perhaps a lot more adults. If your children are in a poorly supervised school, either change schools or fight to get the school administrators to properly protect all of the students with more adult supervision. Aside from changing schools or organizing with other parents to force schools to improve, there is little parents can do to protect their children when free time on campus is unstructured and unsupervised.

To get your children to do their homework, set up a schedule that you can enforce, and have your children study in a location that is easy to monitor, has plenty of flat space to stack books on, and is well lighted. That usually means the kitchen or dining room table. Be there to get them started. Check their assignment books or daily planners for the homework assignments, make sure they understand the material, and then periodically check to make sure they understand what they are doing, and that they stay on task. Do this every night, giving them the amount of monitoring they need. Within a very few weeks they will, for the most part, be doing their homework and studying on their own with minimum supervision, but you will never completely stop checking their progress.

If you are just starting out and you have an uncooperative, temperamentally difficult child, be prepared to do one of two things. Either place a short, almost unbreakable pencil in his or her hand and "help" the child write—it doesn't have to be neat, or even legible—or wait the child out. Children have to sit at the table until they do their work or until you go to bed. They can't sleep, rest, watch TV, listen to the radio, or talk to others. If they don't do their work tonight, start again tomorrow night. Do not lecture, nag, or otherwise provoke the kids to argue with you. If they try, deflect and sponge their arguments: "Regardless of how stupid I may be, finish the assignment now."

When you take the children by the hand and "help" them write, usually within one or two minutes, they are yelling, "I can do it myself!" And you say, "Okay, go ahead." Unless you have a history of giving up and giving in when your children defy you, even difficult kids will normally start doing their work within one or two hours, although some will hold out for as much as three or four hours. If your children have been trained to outwait you because you have frequently given in and given up, they may resist for two or even three days, but if you are consistent and don't give in this time, they will eventually do their schoolwork. If you have a family member or friend who could help you, it would speed things up considerably.

A high degree of resistance on your children's part may be symptomatic of a learning disability, negative peer influences, or a serious gap in their earlier education. Or it could be the result of emotionally frustrating school experiences that were deeply embedded on the children's behavioral templates years before. If there has been a history of poor school performance, or if testing has revealed a learning disability, please consider hiring an experienced, patient, caring, yet firm tutor. Such a person can make all the difference in the world. If you can't afford a professional tutor, call a local college or university student-employment office and see if you can get an inexpensive but patient, caring, and firm student to tutor your child. And if that doesn't work out, call the education department at the college or university and ask if they have an internship program that might meet your children's needs. If nothing else, be prepared to do the tutoring yourself.

A high degree of resistance to education may also warrant a medical evaluation to determine whether drug treatment for attention deficit disorder is appropriate.

Finally, one of the most important things you can do to increase the likelihood of academic success for your children is to keep them away from kids with anti-school, antiauthority attitudes and values. Do your best to get your children involved in after-school activities—football, yearbook staff, senior variety show, school newspaper staff—where most of the college-bound students are, and where there is a great deal of adult involvement and supervision.

CONSISTENCY

Because you must depend on others who are frequently inconsistent, you must be as consistent as possible when it comes to school-related issues. Follow through every single time your children cut class or engage in serious misbehavior at school, and spend the next day at school with them. If they believe you will be there whenever your presence is needed, they will make sure it's not needed.

If you are consistent in enforcing homework schedules, your children will consistently follow those schedules. If you don't have a schedule, you are training your children to put off doing their homework until you remind them. And if you typically forget about homework, many children, especially temperamentally difficult children, will forget right along with you.

- If your children are problem students and you don't clearly set out their homework schedules, with written job descriptions, which you can get from a "how to study" book, they won't do it on their own.
- If your children are problem students and you don't follow through and monitor their homework and classroom work, they won't do it for you.
- If your children are problem students and you aren't consistent about enforcing your rules about homework, classwork, studying, and truancy, your children won't be consistent about obeying them.

Sex

When parents of temperamentally difficult children are asked to establish rules concerning their children's sexual behavior, like other parents, most are hard-pressed to do so. They are confused about what rules are appropriate, although some expect their children to abstain from sex until marriage or at least until adulthood. But few parents actually lay out specific rules concerning sex for their children. They may give advice, they may provide sex education, they may pray, but they rarely set rules governing sex, and they almost never enforce those rules that do exist. Most parents, unfortunately, have no understanding of the actual nature and scope of the sexual world in which their children live.

Tragically, for everyone involved, many difficult kids and their associates are sexually indiscriminate. Unsupervised temperamentally difficult boys who are sexually aggressive, frequently stick themselves into everything from tree stumps and cantaloupes to dogs, ponies, and chickens. They also have sex with each other and, sadly, with vulnerable and easily victimized younger and handicapped children, often within their own families. Sexually aggressive foster children of both sexes often lure other foster children, as well as the innocent and frequently naive children of their foster families, into sexual experiences that will affect them for a lifetime. Poorly supervised juvenile halls, residential treatment centers, and group homes have chronic problems with sexually aggressive children engaging other kids in same-gender sex. One charismatic girl promoting same-gender sex, can, within two to four weeks, convert an entire wing of promiscuous heterosexual juvenile-hall girls (known to each other as "sluts") to declare themselves to be lesbians. One eager young criminal who served time not long ago in a poorly supervised group home on the east slope of the Sierra Nevada, orally copulated with all of the boys in the program repeatedly for more than six months.

The more freedom difficult children have, and the earlier they are released from responsible adult supervision, the greater the likelihood of every type of sexual experience, including rape and molestation, incest, voluntary sex with adults and other children, and the sexual pursuit of weaker children. Many of these children will habituate their early sexual experiences on their behavioral templates to use for a lifetime. Again the underclass children in the inner cities are hardest hit because they are raised in badly structured ethological milieus controlled by the toughest street kids.

Many of the women and girls interviewed by Leon Dash in southeast Washington, D.C., reported early and sometimes frequent rape, molestation, and incest. It's common for boys to be molested, too. One preschool-age boy brought to Dash's attention would cry whenever he wasn't allowed to have oral sex with his mother's live-in boyfriend, as the man had trained him to do (*When Children Want Children*, 1989). The boy was ultimately removed from his mother's home and placed in foster care because she refused to kick the boyfriend out. Heaven help the other children in the foster homes in which such children are placed, as it is common for each sexually aggressive child to introduce dozens of other unsupervised children to sex.

The majority of Americans who will contract the AIDS virus over the next ten years are currently under twenty-one years old; most, in fact, are under eighteen. Many of them will come down with the disease even though they will use condoms. But the majority of young people can be spared the anguish and early death associated with AIDS. Apart from intravenous drug users and their sexual partners, most new cases of AIDS will be acquired by having anal sex with an infected person. In fact, excluding drug users, if men and boys who have sex with one another abstain from anal sex, the likelihood of them contracting the AIDS virus is low, even if their partners are infected. In vaginal sex, women and girls are at higher risk for contracting the disease than men, but if they don't have anal sex, or sex with intravenous drug users or promiscuous men, especially men who engage in anal sex, their risk of contracting the AIDS virus is also low. However, according to research reported in the *Journal of the American Medical Association*, women who have anal and vaginal sex with HIV-positive men are two and one-half times more likely to contract AIDS than women who have only vaginal sex with HIV-positive men ("Male to Female Transmission of Human Immunodeficiency Virus," 14 [Aug. 1987], 525–26). Of course, risk levels go down further if sexual partners consistently use condoms.

Most of the young people who acquire AIDS over the next ten years will be impulsive, immature risk-takers. And many of them will be under the influence of alcohol or drugs when they have sex and will use even less judgment than usual. To make matters worse for young men and boys at risk for contracting AIDS in the future, many uninfected gay men feel left out, abandoned, and socially isolated. They live in a social milieu where having AIDS is synonymous with being gay, and they are *intentionally* joining the rolls of the infected by giving up on safe sex. According to an article in the *Los Angeles Times Magazine* (July 25, 1993), the sex clubs in

California, closed for a decade because of their role in the transmission of AIDS, are open again, and many men are engaging in condom-free anal sex with friends and strangers alike, making life doubly dangerous for new members of the gay community. Worse yet, several of the young men interviewed for the magazine article reported engaging in unprotected anal sex with dozens to hundreds of strangers. A 1991 study by the San Francisco Department of Public Health "found that gay men between the ages of seventeen and twenty-five consistently engaged in high-risk sex. And the younger the men, the riskier the behavior." Tragically, the study also found that even though they all knew about the risk of AIDS and about the increased protection afforded by condoms, "the younger kids, who had less time to get infected, produced an HIV rate almost 40 percent higher than their older counterparts." But even those who are conscientious about using condoms are still at risk if they engage in anal sex with infected persons. Condom failure rates, depending on a number of factors, are between 14 and 25 percent and higher, and even if they wear condoms 100 percent of the time, boys and young men who engage in anal sex with dozens or hundreds of potentially HIV-infected men are doomed.

Now, more than at any other time in history, it is vital that parents set and enforce the rules and standards for their children's sexual behavior. Children's lives depend on it. Unfortunately, many parents, either because they are embarrassed or because they are unsure of their values, frequently don't set or enforce rules or standards for sex. And if parents don't set limits, there can be no rules or firm standards against sexual aggression ("Nice tits, babe. Wanna fuck?"); having sex while infected with a sexually transmitted disease; participating in anal sex (the surest way to transmit disease because of ripping and tearing); gang bangs (several boys with one girl); group sex; sex with a mentally retarded girl who will do anything for friendship, or joining a game to see which boy can seduce the most girls, the ugliest girl, or the fattest girl. Parents need to decide if it is okay for boys to "sow their wild oats" with as many girls and women as they want and, if so, how young the girls can be—fourteen, eleven, eight? And is it okay for liberated girls to drop their pants for any good-looking hunk who comes along? Are girls and boys to have sex only with those they truly love? Can boys frequent prostitutes? Can they become street hustlers themselves? Are both boys and girls to abstain from sex until they are married?

Or just girls? Or neither? May girls have sex as long as they don't get pregnant, or is it okay even if they get pregnant?

If parents don't set the standards and rules for their children's sexual behavior, the kids will set their own, and more often than not, those standards will be set with the help of movies, music, television, and, especially, their peers. In setting standards of sexual behavior parents need to consider the risk of pregnancy, AIDS, and other sexually transmitted diseases, and the effect that sexual relationships will have on students' grades.

Please note that all of these sample rules tell children to do or not do something. They don't allow room for choice. They must be followed, as stated.

SAMPLE RULES

(Some of these rules are inconsistent with one another. Please select those that come closest to the values you wish your children to follow, or revise the sample rules to suit your family. Please use your children's behavior as a guide for setting rules. Not all children, obviously, need to be told to never have sex with an animal. But some do.)

- Never touch anyone's private parts, never let anyone touch yours, and always tell Mom or Dad if someone tries, even if the person threatens to kill or harm you or threatens to kill or harm Mom and Dad.
- Until you are married, don't engage in any type of sexual behavior.
- Unless you are married, always wear a condom or make sure your partner wears a condom.
- When you grow up and take a husband or wife, always remain faithful and loyal. Never have sex outside of your marriage.
- Have sex only with someone you love and respect.
- Until you are an adult and out on your own, don't engage in any type of sexual behavior. Once you are an adult you may use your own judgment, but always treat your sex partners with respect and caring.
- Never force yourself on a woman. If she says no, stop. Never grab or poke a woman's breasts or any other part of her body.

Never stare at a girl's or woman's breasts or bottom at school, at work, or at any other place.
- Never have any kind of sex with children or animals.
- Never engage in recreational sex, including gang bangs and other types of group sex or public sex.
- Never engage in anal sex. Never let anyone put anything, including their penis, fingers, hands, lips, or tongue in your anus, and never put anything into anyone else's.
- Do not go steady or have a girlfriend or boyfriend until you have graduated from high school.
- You may not go out on dates until you demonstrate a consistent level of trust and responsibility, and you may not date at all until you are fifteen (or sixteen) years old.

SUPERVISION

Stopping and Preventing Sexual Behavior: In the past, even the recent past, when many young men and women married and had babies right out of high school or even before graduating from high school, dating and going steady at fifteen, sixteen, or seventeen years old made sense. Dating, going steady, graduating from high school, getting engaged, getting married, having sex, and giving birth—not necessarily in that order—were all wrapped up together. Today, although most couples don't marry until their mid-twenties, it is still common for children to start dating, going steady, and having sex at fifteen, sixteen, or seventeen. And the earlier children start dating, the greater the likelihood of sexual behavior (*Has Sex Education Failed Our Teenagers?* 1990). Some children whose parents allow them to start dating or going steady early are making babies at twelve and thirteen years old.

There is no way around it, when teenagers, or even preteens, start dating regularly, especially when they pair up as girlfriend and boyfriend, or go steady, the likelihood of sex between them increases dramatically (*Sex and the American Teenager,* 1985). It also increases when children closely associate with sexually active children, and when they join or associate with sexually active peer cultures or social cliques. And no matter how many safe-sex classes children take, no matter how many condoms their schools or parents hand out, many of them still won't protect themselves, especially impulsive, immature kids and kids who are under the influence of alcohol or drugs. It is far easier to structure children not to have sex than it is to make sure they use condoms.

Children's sexual relationships dramatically increase the likelihood of reduced school effort and performance, as the kids pay more attention to each other than to school. They also tend to withdraw emotionally from the family and from other activities to concentrate on each other. Difficult children with a tendency toward impulsive behavior and emotional immaturity are especially likely to become preoccupied and even obsessed with a boyfriend or girlfriend. In some instances, the emotional attachment difficult children feel for each other in sexual relationships is more addictive than heroin or rock cocaine. Girls in these emotionally powerful relationships are frequently highly susceptible to accommodating their boyfriends' violence, anger, and need to control. Many of them habituate the behavior patterns experienced in these destructive relationships on their behavior templates to be repeated throughout their adult lives.

If you wish to reduce the likelihood of your children being involved in sexual behavior and the emotionally powerful relationships that frequently go with it, don't let them go steady or have boyfriend-girlfriend relationships, or to associate with kids that do. When they are mature enough (almost never before fifteen or sixteen years old) to start dating, limit their dates with any one person to four times, maximum. To do that, parents obviously need to know and approve of the boys and girls their children are dating. Also, always know and approve of where they are and what they are doing.

CONSISTENCY

Be as consistent as possible in enforcing the rules regarding sex, peers, and dating. Children who have shown themselves to be generally untrustworthy and irresponsible shouldn't date at all. And if your children have a history of sexual misbehavior, if they are sexually precocious or promiscuous, or if they have had sex with other children or with their brothers or sisters or as prostitutes, they must be supervised closely and consistently.

Some parents reading this section will be unwilling to place limitations on their children's dating behavior. If you wish to give your difficult children more freedom and place them at higher risk for the consequences of sexual behavior, that is your prerogative as a parent. But please remember that by a wide margin American children already lead the industrialized world in out-of-marriage pregnancies, abortions, live births, and single-parent households. The greater the freedom, the greater the risk. And please keep these facts in mind:

- If you don't clearly establish your rules, your children and their friends will set their own rules.
- If you don't follow through and enforce your rules, your children and their friends won't do it for you.
- If you aren't consistent about enforcing your rules, your children won't be consistent about obeying them.

8

JASON, EDDY, JULIE, BONITA, AND NICOLE REVISITED

Jason After Back in Control Training

Jason knocked his mother to the floor as she tried to keep him from leaving the house to join his gangster friends. As he left, she told him he was under arrest, and then she called the police. She followed the script I had helped her write in the Back in Control class, and when the first officer arrived and told her there was nothing he could do, she said, "I arrested my son for criminal battery. Under California law I can arrest anyone who commits a crime in my presence or against me, and you are required to effect that arrest, write the report, and take the suspect into custody. If you refuse, you can be arrested."

She said the same thing to the patrol sergeant who came out to back up the original patrol officer, and to the watch commander, and to the deputy chief who called the probation department, which gave permission for Jason to be brought in to juvenile hall.

After his mother got the cooperation she demanded, Jason tried to use his well-practiced act of physical intimidation and violence against the police and probation officers who placed him in custody. But he wound up restrained on the floor, face down and handcuffed, with more than four hundred pounds of cops on top of him. When he kicked an older female probation officer who attempted to remove the handcuffs at juvenile hall, he again found himself restrained with almost six hundred pounds of cops and probation officers on top of him. And when he refused to walk down the hall to the boys' receiving unit, he was carried, still handcuffed, by two large probation officers. He spent two more hours sitting on a bench in the boys' receiving unit before he calmed down enough so that the handcuffs could be removed and he could go to bed. The next morning, when he was given the choice of getting out of bed on his own or getting help from the staff, he chose to get up cooperatively.

For the first time in his life, Jason actually had to obey someone's orders, and he didn't like it. He felt he had lost control. The rules in juvenile hall were mandatory. He had no choice but to obey them. And when he learned that the only way he could get out of juvenile hall quickly was to convince his parents to take him home, he underwent a profound attitude adjustment. When his mother came to visit him later that afternoon she was welcomed by a boy who had a new appreciation of her authority and power, especially after she made it clear that if he touched her in the future he would go right back through the booking room door. She also let him know what the rules would be when he got home. She told him that he was out of the gang and that he was never to dress like a gangster, look like a gangster, or act like a gangster again. She also told him that he was not to associate with any gangsters or other criminals and that he would be kept busy at home and at school to make sure he didn't have the time to mix with the neighborhood gangsters. And finally she told him that she had gone through his room and removed all of his gang clothing and paraphernalia.

Since arguing and violence were the only techniques that Jason had ever needed to rely on, his mother, using the Back in Control Parenting Program, had little trouble regaining control over his behavior, even without her husband's support—something she was never able to get. And with no emotional support from his gangster friends, Jason quickly calmed down. When his mother told him to stay home, he stayed home. When he tried to engage her in an argument, she deflected and sponged his provocations. He didn't like it, and he frequently thought his mother was being more than unfair. But she was consistent in enforcing her rules and in reaching out to Jason with affection. She got him involved in church youth activities, and in a search and rescue unit run by a local Boy Scouts of America Explorer group. Within a few weeks Jason was not only behaving well, he was pleasant to live with again. He hasn't hit his mother since his trip to juvenile hall.

Eddy After Back in Control

It is fascinating to find situations where dangerous misbehavior—in this case alcohol abuse—is easier to stop than the violent behavior that children use to thwart parents' efforts to regain control. In this case, once Eddy's Mom learned how to control his violent tantrums, everything else fell into place, including the end to his drinking.

Eddy's Mom almost immediately started using what she learned in the Back in Control workshop. On the evening following her first session she tried to get Eddy to sit down at the kitchen table to do his spelling homework, but he tried to duck out the front door to go drinking with his friends. When stopped, he went on a rampage, yelling and cursing, shoving the kitchen table against the wall, and knocking over chairs. As he tried to run out the back door, his mother grabbed him around the waist, put him on the floor, pinned his flailing arms to his chest, and wrapped her legs around his kicking legs. As soon as she had him physically under control, she started calmly repeating over and over again, "Calm down, honey, calm down. As soon as you calm down and you're ready to do your homework, I'll let go of you. Calm down, honey. I love you."

Eddy cursed, wriggled, twisted, and turned, doing everything he could to get away from his mother. But no matter how many times he tried to escape her grip and screamed "Fuck you," "I hate you," or "Get your fat ass off of me," she kept repeating, "Calm down, honey, calm down. As soon as you calm down and you're ready to do your homework, I'll let go of you. Calm down. I love you."

It took Eddy forty minutes to use up most of his excess energy. He finally relaxed his muscles and calmed down.

"Are you ready to do your homework now?" his mother asked.

"Uh-huh," he replied quietly. Then, as soon as he felt her grip relaxing, he tried to jerk his hands and feet free. But he was quickly enveloped once again within his mother's arms and legs, and he stayed wrapped up for another twenty minutes, until he had expended his last reserve of energy. A little more than an hour after throwing the tantrum and refusing to do his homework, Eddy was seated at the kitchen table, doing his spelling assignment with his mother's help.

The next day Mom secured the doors with double-key dead-bolt locks to prevent Eddy from sneaking out. Over the following two months Eddy had to be held seven times to prevent his violent tantrums from getting out of control. Each "holding" took less time than the previous one. The seventh time Eddy had to be held for only five minutes before he calmed down and did as he had been told; it was also his last attempt to throw a violent tantrum.

During the first month of the Back in Control program Eddy's Mom spent one day in school with him to help his female teacher regain control. She cut off his association with his drinking and smoking buddies, the neighborhood street toughs, by getting him back into after-school activities and sports, and both she and Eddy got involved in community theater. Within two months Eddy was basically following his mother's rules most of the time with moderate supervision and monitoring. He had no opportunity to use alcohol or tobacco, and all of the ethological milieus in which he was spending his time were alcohol- and tobacco-free. A year later he had the best grades in the seventh grade, was on the soccer and Little League all-star teams, and, like his mother, had a speaking role in a community theater production. And best of all, Eddy's violence had been replaced with a loving, affectionate relationship with his mother. His condescending attitude toward women had disappeared, and he was no longer likely to hurt the women who show up later in his life. He was no longer his drunken father's son.

Julie After Back in Control

Regaining control of an out-of-control child takes a lot of time, energy, and determination, and one of the most difficult tasks parents face is the challenge of removing runaway teenage girls from the grip of a controlling, manipulative young man to whom they are emotionally bonded—even when the young man is violent and physically abusive to the girl.

To ensure that parents have enough strength and determination to regain control of their misbehaving children, one of our requirements is that the children must attend the Back in Control workshops with their parents, voluntarily or otherwise. (Our experience is that if parents can get their kids to the workshops, they can usually do everything else that is necessary to regain control.) We make an exception to this rule only if the child is presently a runaway and not available to attend the workshop. In those cases parents come to the initial workshop alone to learn how to find their runaway children, and then bring them to the next workshop.

At her first session, fourteen-year-old Julie had been picked up by her father that morning, and she was angry. She refused to leave the family car until the Back in Control trainer, at her parents' request, told her, "Julie, you're going to get out of the car. The only question is whether you do it on your own, which your parents and I would certainly prefer, or you do it with our assistance. It's up to you."

The trainer asked the parents to wait by the open passenger-side door while he walked around to open the other door. He waited a moment, but as soon as he reached in to help Julie out of the car she got out and rushed into the workshop center to avoid being "helped" in.

That evening, after the trainer had helped the parents set up a supervision structure to keep Julie away from her boyfriend, Sean, the family went home, and Julie's parents followed through as the trainer had suggested. They secured Julie's bedroom window so she could not climb out. They placed a small portable motion-sensor alarm in the hallway outside her bedroom door so she couldn't sneak out of her room during the night unnoticed. (As an alternative, they could have moved her temporarily into their bedroom, or they could have slept in her room with her.) They installed a double-key dead-bolt lock on the outside door. They checked the smoke detectors to make sure the batteries were good, and they set up a fire-escape plan to ensure that everyone, including Julie, could get out of the house if there was an emergency. They disconnected all of the telephones, relying on voice mail to take any messages and a pager to notify them of urgent calls. (This may seem like an incredible expenditure of time, effort, and money, but keep in mind that these are loving parents who wish to protect their fourteen-year-old child from the sex, violence, and machinations of a nineteen-year-old unemployed high school dropout who is doing his best to drag their daughter down to his level and keep her there.)

The following Monday, Julie's father asked for and received a restraining order from the municipal court directing Sean to stay away from Julie. He also wrote a letter to Sean:

> As you know, our daughter Julie, a minor child, has been with you when she was a truant from school and when she was a runaway from her home. This is to notify you that from now on anytime she is with you, or is at any place under your control, while she is truant from school, or while she is a runaway, you will be contributing to her delinquency and subject to arrest. And unless you receive our permission in advance for her to be with you, you are to assume she is a runaway.
>
> We ask for your cooperation in this matter. Please make no attempt to communicate with Julie or otherwise undercut the authority or rules of our home.

One copy of the letter was sent to Sean by certified mail, return receipt requested, and another copy was sent to him via first class mail, so that Sean would have a difficult time denying that he had received the letter. The parents had also been told to keep a record of any contact between Sean and Julie so they could build a potential criminal case against Sean for contributing to the delinquency of a minor.

Julie was well supervised by her parents, family friends, and relatives twenty-four hours a day for more than two months, and for one three-week stretch, her father took her out of state to spend time with her grandparents in Mississippi. When she got back, she was enrolled in an independent study program where she did all of her studies at home, supervised by her parents. Her old friends were invited over a few at a time to visit. She was also reintroduced to her music (the piano). And, most important, in addition to sharing love and affection with her parents, Julie was spending more and more time away from Sean's powerful controlling influence.

Three months after starting the Back in Control program, Julie was enrolled at a public school with a closed campus and a good communication system between school and home. As she did well and earned more trust, she was given increased levels of freedom. But based on her susceptibility to a dangerous young man like Sean, it would be a long time before her parents again took her supervision for granted.

Bonita After Back in Control

After attending the initial all-day Back in Control workshop with Bonita, her mother immediately reiterated her rule prohibiting sex until Bonita was finished with her college education and ready for marriage. And because of the vital importance of removing her from an ethological milieu that promoted and even demanded early casual and dangerous sex, Bonita's mother established a rule that her daughter not associate with any of her new neighborhood friends. She backed up the rule by requiring that Bonita come home directly after school, that she not leave the house without permission, and that she not use the telephone without permission. Mom and Grandma both helped supervise Bonita to make sure she followed these new rules. Then Mom rearranged Bonita's days so that she spent most of her time in an adult-supervised, adult-directed environment. She received permission from the city school district to transfer Bonita back to her old school, where the peer pressure to engage in early sex was much weaker, where the adult supervision much stronger, and where none of her old friends would badger her into having sex. She also enrolled Bonita in a well-supervised after-school day-care program run by the YMCA.

Even though they continued to live at Grandma's house for financial reasons, from then on, Mom consistently made sure that Bonita spent her time in adult-directed ethological milieus, including the one at home, which encouraged academic success, personal responsibility, hard work, chastity, and sobriety. As a result, Bonita is in the top 10 percent of her high school graduating class, with a combined 1150 on the SAT, and she has been accepted at the University of California at Los Angeles, Howard University, and Spelman College. Tragically, most of the neighborhood girls who pushed Bonita into early sex have given birth—some of them twice—and dropped out of high school to care for their children. None of them are married, and few are receiving dependable financial support from their children's fathers.

Nicole After Back in Control

Nicole's parents were confronted by a highly experienced, well-entrenched school-hater whose behavioral templates were all focused on how to avoid doing schoolwork and on getting parents and teachers to leave her alone. To get her to habituate good study habits and to change her focus from school failure to school success would require more concentrated and determined work than anything her parents had ever done, but after the initial Back in Control workshop they were confident that they could do it.

They bought an inexpensive daily planner and told Nicole to write down everything that was assigned in every class. Her homework assignments were to be written in detail every day, including the due dates, and she was to get signatures from every teacher confirming the truthfulness of what she wrote. If she had no homework, she was told to have the teachers write "no homework." Meetings were set up with Nicole's teachers to coordinate what was going on at school with what her parents would be doing at home.

A daily study schedule was set up. Because her reading level was three years behind her grade level, a thirty-minute reading period with parents started her schedule off at five-thirty. At six she would do the homework assigned by her first-period English teacher, followed in order by the homework from her other classes. Because of the high level of resistance they expected from Nicole, her parents planned on limiting her homework to her first-period class for the first several days. Once she was somewhat cooperative, they would gradually add more. But she was far from cooperative those first few nights.

All she had to do that first night was write her ten assigned English vocabulary words five times each, or until she could spell and define them correctly. But she used her full repertoire of avoidance skills and techniques in an attempt to wear her parents down and avoid doing what should have been a ten-minute homework assignment. She argued ("I'm stupid." "I can't do it." "You can't make me do it." "This is stupid." "The teacher doesn't want us to do it this way." "I already learned this"). She lied ("I already did this at school." "I already turned this in." "This is an extra credit project; it doesn't have to be turned in." "The teacher changed his mind and said we don't have to do this assignment"). She cursed her parents

and called them names ("You're both assholes." "Fuck your home-
work, and fuck you, too." "Go to hell." "You're a fucking whore").
She feigned illness ("I have a headache." "I'm going to throw up."
"I've got diarrhea." "I have cramps").

She also walked away from the kitchen table several times, only
to be brought back by her parents every time. She locked herself in
the bathroom, but her parents used a key to open it (and then took
the locking handle off the door) and brought her back to the table.
Once she threw herself on the floor in a tantrum and was held
firmly until she calmed down.

Her parents took turns serving as the primary homework monitor and supervisor, but whenever she became too much for one of
them to handle, the other would immediately be there for support
and follow-through. At a little past two in the morning on that first
night she finally spelled and defined her ten vocabulary words. Her
parents praised her, and everyone went to bed. The next night she
finished her homework at a little before midnight; the night after
that she completed it at eleven. Within six weeks, homework was no
longer a fighting issue with Nicole, and there was a clear improve-
ment in her reading ability. Her poor classroom behavior and her
truancy, however, continued until Nicole was walked class to class
by her mom on two different occasions immediately following two
different class cuts, and until Dad sat with her in three classes to
make sure she behaved well and did her classroom assignments.
The teacher of one of those classes could not control his students, so
Nicole was transferred to a stronger, more discipline-conscious
teacher for that subject. Mom also took Nicole to school twice and
went to each of her teachers after Nicole "forgot" to get the teachers'
homework confirmation signatures on her daily planner.

By the end of that quarter Nicole was receiving the best grades of
her life, with nothing under a C. During the second semester of her
ninth grade year she was pulled out of the remedial education
classes in which she had initially been enrolled and placed in a
college-prep curriculum. At the end of her sophomore year she had
earned a 3.0 grade-point average and was well on her way to
college.

9

THE SUCCESS CONTINUES

Attachment and Bonding

The most important element in creating a bond between parents and children is simply being there. In general, the more time you spend with your children the closer they will be to you. Especially if some of that time is spent talking together, laughing with one another, or enjoying activities together. Even doing household chores together can be a bonding experience.

Parents who are actively involved in their children's activities almost always form a strong and lasting bond, unless negative peers or other outsiders step in to pull children away from their families. Dads and Moms who coach their children's basketball, soccer, softball, or swim teams build a strong bond. Parents who attend all of their children's dance, piano, or singing recitals and drive them around town or from town to town for competitions or auditions create a strong bond with their children. Parents who always have their cameras out and their photo albums open, showing their children off to family and friends with pride, build a strong bond.

Parents who frequently tell their children that they are loved build a strong bond with their children. So do parents who hug and touch their children, including teenagers.

Parents who are consistent and who follow through and enforce their rules maintain and enhance the bond they have created with their children. Inconsistency damages everything it touches, including parent-child relationships. Love that is not dependable, that can't be counted on is worse than no love at all. Parents who are always angry because their children didn't do as they were told damage the bond they have built with their children. Nagging, rather than monitoring, produces anger for everyone in a parent-child relationship. And arguing does more harm to parent-child relationships than anything short of the damage caused by negative peers.

Parents whose children form a strong attachment to negative peers often feel their children being pulled away from them emotionally as well as physically. And few things can cripple a parent's bond with a child faster than the pervasive, angry "up yours" attitude of children who are bonded to negative peers or other negative influences. If you are in such a situation, do everything you can to remove your children from their negative peers or delinquent subcultures.

In fact, everything in this book is designed to rebuild the bond between parent and child. Being specific and clear, so there is no doubt about the rules ("Honey, take off your shoes now and put them on the throw rug next to the door; do that every time you come in from now on"), improves the parent-child bond. So do daily schedules and routines.

Not using punishment also enhances parent-child attachment, as does making sure that children succeed in their everyday activities. No child will need to fail at school if parents know how to structure their children's academic success so that the children will go into the classroom prepared, ready to answer any question their teachers throw at them. These children will feel good at the moment and also when it comes time to study that night with Mom or Dad.

Being Involved

One of the primary reasons so many American children are out of control and so many homes, schools, and communities are chaotic, is the reduction of adult authority and structure in children's lives. Most American institutions concerned about difficult children, especially the family, have had their authority to structure children's behavior weakened by social and economic forces that are beyond their control. Over the past thirty years their authority has also been intentionally weakened by those who oppose authority-based hierarchies, especially parental authority.

Many liberal parenting professionals and therapists see children as one more group "victimized" by American society. They either deny that parents—or any adults, for that matter—have the ability to structure, form, or mold children's behavior; or, worse, they believe that parental authority is inherently corrupt and should be weakened or eliminated. They want children to have the freedom to live their lives as they please, without parental intervention.

In the 1960s and 1970s educational and social critic John Holt, who had no children of his own, argued that children of any age should have full adult rights including the right to vote, the right to make contracts, the right to privacy (no snoopy parents checking on homework or drugs), the right to full welfare benefits, and the right to live wherever they please, including the streets, without parental permission or interference (*Escape from Childhood*, 1974, pp. 1–2). He saw no reason to force them to go to school or to study. His primary concern was to help the "oppressed" child find "some way of resisting or escaping whatever pressures his parents may put on him" (p. 113). Holt saw all parents as self-serving slave masters, regardless of how loving, or caring they might be.

> For a very long time, ever since men formed societies in which some people bossed others, children have fulfilled this very important function. Every adult parent, however lowly or powerless, had at least someone he could command, threaten, and punish. No man was so poor, even a slave, that he could not have these few slaves of his own. Today, when most "free" men feel like slaves, having their own home-grown slaves is very satisfying. Many could not do without them (pp. 48–49).

The idea of children raising themselves without parental authority goes back two centuries to the writings of Jean-Jacques Rousseau, who abandoned his own children to an orphanage. It shows up again in the work of some of late twentieth-century America's most influential "parenting experts," including therapists Thomas Gordon, author of *Parent Effectiveness Training (P.E.T.)*, and Don Dinkmeyer and Gary McKay, authors of *Systematic Training for Effective Parenting (S.T.E.P.)*. Gordon clearly sets out his views on the inherent weakness of parental authority and power when he writes,

"It is paradoxical but true that parents lose influence by using power and will have more influence on their children by giving up their power or refusing to use it" Parent Effectiveness Training [P.E.T.], 1970, p. 192; (emphasis in original).

Gordon also believes parents are incapable of stopping their children from smoking, having sex, or refusing to do their homework. He goes on as follows:

> Other behaviors can be added to our list of things that parents may have no power to change. Heavy makeup, drinking, getting into trouble at school, associating with certain kids, having dates with members of another race or religion, smoking grass, and so on. All a parent can do is to try to influence by being a model, being an effective consultant, and developing a "therapeutic" relationship with the kids. After that, what else? As I see it, a parent can only accept the fact that he ultimately has no power to prevent such behavior, if the child is bent on doing them (pp. 279–80).

Dinkmeyer and McKay try to dispose of parental authority by denying its existence, telling their readers or clients that "a parent can't really force his or her will on a teenager, and a teenager can't really force his or her will on a parent" (*Systematic Training for Effective Parenting of Teens* [STEP/Teen], 1983, p. 6). But, as any overwhelmed victim of childhood badgering knows, some children are quite good at forcing their will on others. And even Dinkmeyer and McKay, after denying the effectiveness of parental authority, reverse themselves and admit that parents can successfully get children to follow the rules of their homes and schools, but they add, "The parents appear to have 'won.' But what is the price of victory? We believe the price is too high if teenagers lose their self-respect and learn to please and conform rather than think for themselves and make informed decisions." In other words as long as children do their own thinking and come to their own independent conclusions, they can do virtually anything they feel like doing.

Now, before you say, "That can't be right. No therapist with common sense is going to encourage children to do whatever they please," read what Daniel Mason, another antiauthoritarian psychotherapist specializing in adolescent drug and alcohol abuse, advocates: "Healthy and unhealthy teens need to be encouraged to experiment [with alcohol, drugs, and sex], and then process their experiments." And he goes on to add, "We ought to hope that they do. If they don't, they aren't learning their own healthy values for later in life" (*Double Duty: Parenting Our Kids While Reparenting Ourselves*, 1990, p. 198).

The goal of liberal antiauthoritarian therapists is not to have children obey their parents or conform to household, school, or community rules, even though that is what parents are usually paying the therapist to do, but instead to free children from adult authority and responsibility and empower them to make their own decisions. These therapists commonly tell parents to compromise and negotiate conflicts with their out-of-control children—as if incorrigible children are going to voluntarily give up any of the power they have already wrested away from their parents—or else they encourage parents to back out of conflicts with their children and give them the "freedom to fail." Even though virtually all of the research on school success has found an overwhelmingly strong link between academic achievement and the level of parental involvement in all aspects of children's schooling, especially homework, Dinkmeyer and McKay advocate that parents back off:

> We believe that school is the teen's job, not the parents'. Parents may buy school materials, provide educational opportunities, and offer an attentive ear. But it's best that they not supervise homework, pry into their teenager's life at school, or set up a system of reward and punishment for grades. All of these actions will backfire sooner or later. Why? Because through them teens learn how to please or disappoint their parents, not themselves (*STEP/Teen*), p. 33).

On one very important point Dinkmeyer and McKay are right. Children who are bonded and emotionally attached to their parents frequently follow rules for that reason alone.

Every time a therapist successfully persuades parents to abdicate or share parental authority, the center of power within the parent-child relationship shifts from the parent to the child, from structure to chaos. And if parents listen to the advice of those democratic therapists influenced by Gordon, Dinkmeyer, and McKay and quit "supervising" homework and "prying" into their teenagers' lives at school, they will find that children with a history of poor achievement, impulsivity, and classroom misbehavior, not to mention any number of learning disabilities, will almost immediately use their

newly gained freedom to establish lifelong patterns of school failure. And worse, those parents who actually follow the advice of
Mason and the thousands of drug and alcohol counselors who
share his professional outlook and allow their children to experiment with drugs, alcohol, and sex, will too often find their children
and grandchildren living corrupt and chaotic lives repeatedly
touched by sorrow and death.

Tragically, the beliefs and values shared by Holt, Gordon, Dinkmeyer, and McKay, and Mason go far beyond the mental health
therapy community. Their views on parenting and on what they see
as the corrupting nature of parental authority are also deeply embedded in schools of social work, alcohol and drug treatment training programs, and schools of education. Over the past two decades,
hundreds of thousands of teachers, social workers, probation officers, chemical dependency counselors, mental health therapists,
and others who work with parents and children have been trained
to see parents as either incompetent or corrupt.

There is a highly organized, aggressive political lobby made up
primarily of Planned Parenthood and other pro-choice advocates
that has done its best—and its best is very good—to end parental
authority over every aspect of children's sexual issues. In many
states parents have been all but stripped of their authority to oversee their children's sexual values and behavior. Many medical professionals refuse to tell parents if their children have sexually
transmitted diseases. Schools are handing out condoms without
parental permission or notification, and children can have abortions
without even notifying their parents. And in 1993 a Florida court
dismissed a statutory rape case initiated by a fifteen-year-old girl's
parents because that state's abortion law gives children the right to
privacy in sexual matters.

The same antiauthority pressures that have weakened parental
authority, have also brought changes to America's schools. Before
he unleashed his wrath at parents, John Holt accused teachers and
schools of being exploiters of children. While he saw children as
slaves to their parents, he also saw students as "prisoners" in their
schools (How Children Fail, 1964, p. 97). And even though Holt's
position is extreme, he is not alone. In high schools, junior high
schools, and even some elementary schools, too many teachers
follow the "freedom to fail" policy and knowingly allow their students to fail. "I'm here to teach," the typical proponent of this

dogma says. "If they don't want to learn, that's up to them. I'm not a baby-sitter, and I'm not going to take them by the hand and make sure they do their studies. If they want to fail, that's up to them, too." What this means, in everyday practice, is that many teachers will not monitor, supervise, or otherwise structure difficult or indifferent students, will not say anything to them if they don't turn in their assignments, and will not promptly notify parents of academic problems. Everything is left up to the student, and given that freedom, virtually every temperamentally difficult child will choose to fail.

Schools that relinquish their authority to set and enforce dress codes find that some students will constantly stretch the limits of taste and decency, while the most aggressive and dangerous ones (skinheads, Crips and Bloods, chollas, and others) use the opportunity to recruit new members by wearing distinctive uniforms that reinforce each group's identity and set them apart from the academically oriented students.

Schools that don't consistently and accurately notify parents of all absences and truancies on the day they occur (failure to do so is common at public high schools throughout the United States) purposely limit their authority to keep students in class and deprive parents of theirs. If parents aren't notified of their children's absences it's difficult for them to make sure they stay in class. Schools that don't promptly and consistently notify parents of missed homework assignments, poor test scores, and other indications of academic problems have not only failed to meet their own responsibility but have also prevented parents from fulfilling theirs. If parents aren't promptly informed of misbehavior, academic failure, or attendance problems, many children, especially the most impulsive difficult ones, will take advantage, and chaos will ensue. Schools with open campuses, where children as a matter of policy can come and go as they please, have abdicated virtually all of their authority to keep children on campus and in class. And the children who are at highest risk for school failure, dropping out, drug and alcohol abuse, childhood pregnancy, and criminality are allowed to go off campus, unsupervised, to do as they please.

Parents who are forced to send their children to public schools with open campuses, inadequate supervision, late or undependable notification of truancy or academic failure are severely handicapped in trying to structure their children to do well. In fact, bad schools can undercut all but the most heroic efforts of parents who are trying to regain control of their out-of-control children.

The most persistent enemy of adult authority and structure in public schools and on America's mean and violent streets is the American Civil Liberties Union. The ACLU has consistently fought dress and grooming codes, discipline policies, and supervision procedures in schools. In 1990, when the Detroit public schools were in a crisis of violence, with many students bringing guns, knives, and other weapons to school, and with record numbers of children being wounded and killed at school, the ACLU fought the Detroit school district to stop it from making children walk through metal detectors on their way into their schools. In 1990 in Washington, D.C., when record numbers of children were killing and being killed at the height of the rock-cocaine drug war, the ACLU once again decided it would rather see inner-city children killing each other in the streets than kept home with their families, and it vigorously opposed the city's curfew for children. There are no neighborhoods in the United States more overwhelmed by out-of-control children than those in Washington, D.C., and Detroit.

For most of the twentieth century parents with poorly structured, incorrigible, out-of-control, or violent children could receive support from their local juvenile courts and probation departments just by asking and at no cost. Most of these children were placed in the structured environment of probation supervision and told to mind their parents, go to school, and stay away from kids in trouble. They were also told to report to the probation officer regularly. Most of these kids were never locked up. Even if it was never used, just knowing there was a system with police, probation officers, and juvenile court judges who would support their authority gave many parents the confidence to stand up to temperamentally difficult children. But no longer.

During the 1970s a lobby of liberal, anti-authority children's rights activists, patients' rights activists, and fiscal conservatives successfully pushed to "free" out-of-control children from juvenile halls and also to free the chronically mentally ill from state hospitals. With little forethought and virtually no research into the possible consequences of the legislation, Congress passed and President Ford signed the 1974 Juvenile Justice Act which, through the power of the federal purse, caused state juvenile courts to stop helping parents, schools, and cities with incorrigible, runaway, and truant children. Tens of thousands of the most incorrigible, out-of-control children, unable to properly take care of themselves, were put out on the streets to become prostitutes, drug dealers, criminals, and corpses. At the same time, hundreds of thousands of mentally ill men and women were released and expelled from hospitals and forced onto the streets to become derelicts and drunks, often going unbathed and unfed, ready to be robbed, raped, and brutalized, because liberals wanted them freed and fiscal conservatives wanted to save money. And both groups got their way. Most of today's homeless population is made up of the mentally ill and former out-of-control kids whose behavioral templates were structured for lifetime failure in childhood. Even if drugs and alcohol disappeared from the lives of America's homeless, most of them could not survive on their own without extensive, long-term, restructuring programs. And most of the American prison population consists of young men and women who as teenagers and preteenagers were out of their parents' control, even though, as today, most of their parents asked, begged, and pleaded in vain for assistance from the nation's juvenile courts and probation departments.

Juvenile court support for parents with out-of-control children all but ended with the passage and implementation of the 1974 Juvenile Justice Act, and the United States Supreme Court's *Galt* decision. *Galt* changed the direction of America's juvenile courts from "best interest of the child" to an adversarial forum burdened with attorneys, where the children's best interests are subordinated to plea-bargaining, deal-making, and crowded court calendars.

For many parents, the greatest loss of parental authority originated with the procedural changes in reporting child abuse to child protective agencies. In 1974 Congress passed the Child Abuse Prevention and Treatment Act, which completely revamped the nation's child-protection system. All fifty states passed laws requiring that almost everyone working with children report virtually anything that could possibly be child abuse. Criminal penalties were provided to encourage compliance. At the same time, child-abuse hot lines were established nationwide to take secret reports of suspected abuse from neighbors, family members, ex-husbands, former mothers-in-law, and anyone else with a valid report or a grudge. As a result, hundreds of thousands of additional suspected "abused" or "neglected" children were reported annually. But while the new laws resulted in hundreds of thousands of new marginal and false reports of abuse, few additional cases of serious abuse were uncovered. In some states, the number of actual abuse cases dropped (*U.S. News and World Report*, April 27, 1987, p. 39). In addition to scaring and intimidating millions of parents and children unnecessarily, all the mandatory reporting laws actually accomplished was to divert the attention of tens of thousands of caseworkers away from the serious cases that could have profited from their assistance. Richard Wexler, a newspaper reporter who has written extensively on child-abuse issues, estimates that a minimum of 60 percent of all child abuse reports are false ("Wounded Innocents, The Real Victims of the War against Child Abuse," 1990, p. 87).

Child-abuse laws are written broadly, without clear definition. And police officers and social workers do not have to meet the "probable cause" requirements in criminal law to remove children from their homes; they don't have to have a warrant issued by a judge who has reviewed the evidence; they don't even need the approval of a supervisor. While the final decision is in the hands of a judge, social workers and police officers are left to use their own judgment and values in initially determining whether child abuse or neglect has occurred. And in most jurisdictions no procedures are in place to deal with officials who wrongly remove children from their homes.

Every year hundreds of thousands of innocent parents, along with parents who may have impulsively slapped a child for swearing at them ("What the fuck do you know, bitch?"), or who left a red mark or welt on a child's butt but who have not truly abused their children, are interrogated by caseworkers or police officers and are faced with the pervasive fear of having their children taken away from them. And these fears are fully justified. The threat of removing the children is one of the most successful tools social workers have to get parents, including those who have done nothing wrong, to "voluntarily" enter child-abuse programs. Tragically, many parents, fearing that their out-of-control children will be taken from them, just give up and stop trying to control their behavior.

Please note that the issue here is not the legitimate and necessary protection of children who are beaten, burned, tortured, starved, raped, or abandoned. Nor do we provide support or encouragement for punishing misbehaving children, because, as noted previously, punishment is not an effective way to change behavior. The issue in question is the lack of due process in child-abuse investigations and the resulting sense of fear and persecution produced in parents and children.

After the passage of the 1974 Juvenile Justice Act, and after states stopped their juvenile courts from locking up incorrigible, truant, and runaway children, including chronic drug users, parents with health insurance or a lot of money sought help for their out-of-control children in the only place where the law still allowed children to be held against their will: psychiatric hospital programs. And almost immediately, liberal patients' rights advocates began a campaign to restrict the authority of the programs' doctors and nurses. In many general hospitals, despite the health risk, and even though research shows a strong connection between children smoking tobacco and using drugs, the only place in the whole building where smoking is allowed is on the adolescent chemical dependency wards—because of patients' rights regulations. These same regulations also frequently require that patients be allowed unmonitored access to a telephone. Young drug users, who are often in the program against their will, call their drug-using cronies every day for emotional support and a few laughs. The regulations also often require that teenage patients be allowed to wear their own clothes rather than hospital clothing. Even though these chemically oriented children are supposed to be in a therapeutic milieu, many of them actually spend much of their time in a drug and alcohol–oriented ethological milieu. The result is that teenage drug abusers spend thirty to ninety days dressed in stoner clothes in a drug program with a dozen other stoners, talking to their stoner friends on the telephone, and they leave, unchanged, with their parents or their insurance carrier $35,000 to $100,000 poorer.

Despite continuing liberal efforts to free children from adult authority, there is no evidence that giving children, especially temperamentally difficult children, the authority to make bad decisions on vital matters helps them to become wise or well behaved. In fact, all of the evidence shows the opposite to be true. The research into delinquency, dropping out, drug and alcohol abuse, and teen pregnancy shows that the less parents are involved in their children's lives, the greater the likelihood of children's involvement in crime, school failure, chemical dependency, and pregnancy (*Adolescents at Risk*, 1990, p. 91).

Along with a significant loss of parental authority there has been an even larger and continuing loss in formal and informal structure for children, especially those most at risk for life failures. Police departments, juvenile courts, probation departments, social service agencies, and schools have either withdrawn from their previous responsibilities or have severely limited them—at a time when the need for them is at an all time high.

Those cities that relinquished their authority to enforce children's curfew and school attendance laws found that abandoned authority quickly grabbed by the community's most aggressive, incorrigible, and delinquent children, who now spend even more time together, away from adults, reinforcing each other's negative attitudes and behavior.

Those states that followed the guidelines of the 1974 Juvenile Justice Act and stopped supporting parental authority over "status offenders" (incorrigibles, truants, and runaways) in the juvenile courts found that the number of children involved in crime did not decrease, as had been hoped. Instead, it increased to historic levels. In the inner city where parents had traditionally relied on the juvenile court and probation department for help with incorrigible and out-of-control children, juvenile crime exploded.

If adequate external structure is not provided by families, schools, and government agencies—especially police and social service agencies, juvenile courts, and probation departments—temperamentally difficult children will continue to bring chaos to their communities. Violent crime will continue to increase, great numbers of children will continue to drop out of school, more babies will be born to teenagers, drug use will increase again, our urban centers will continue to decay, and parts of our nation will continue to grow ever more out of control—because unsupervised, poorly structured, temperamentally difficult children form the nucleus of these problems.

Power and authority belong to those that use them, and if adults don't use theirs, the children in their care will. And the children most likely to take control are impulsive, aggressive, persistent, and determined always to get their own way. More than at any other time in this century, parents now have to rely solely on their own resources to regain control of their difficult children. But if this nation is to survive, we need to start rebuilding parental and adult authority to make sure the next generation of parents needn't face antiauthority political obstacles in raising our grandchildren. We need to put parents first.

10

PARENTS IN CONTROL—AT LAST

Restoring Parental Authority and Responsibilities

At one time there were informal parent-support networks made up of parents, neighbors, grandparents, shopkeepers, and the people at school, all of whom helped supervise neighborhood children. To children, the people who knew their parents seemed to be everywhere—next door, down the street, around the corner, and across town. And those people never hesitated to let the children's parents know—sometimes with amazing speed—when their kids did something wrong or when they were hanging around with the wrong crowd. Even the media cooperated. There was nothing children could watch, read, or listen to in the popular media that promoted drugs, gangsters, sex, or crime.

Today, however, the social structures that traditionally looked out for children have collapsed. Almost all of the parents and most of the neighbors are now at work and don't return home until late in the day. Many of the grandparents are in Miami, in Sun City, or in a Winnebago crisscrossing the country, or they are behind locked doors and barred windows, afraid to even sit on their front porches. In the inner city the situation is even worse. Many of the mothers and fathers are missing—incapacitated by alcohol or drugs, or dead—and it's up to the grandmothers and even great-grandmothers to raise the surviving children.

At the same time, those institutions that have historically helped parents with difficult children are less able or unwilling to do so. Police agencies, probation departments, and juvenile courts in most locations no longer back up and assist parents with children who

155

run away, are truant, or are otherwise out of control. In fact, most juvenile courts and probation departments don't even back up and support parents' efforts to discipline or supervise their delinquent and criminal children. Worse yet, juvenile courts and social service agencies in many jurisdictions are seen by parents as their enemies, not their allies. And government-run schools are no longer dependable about educating or, in many instances, even protecting their students.

The Solution: Prevention

CURFEW LAWS

Children under eighteen years old who are out late at night away from adult supervision are at high risk for being both perpetrators and victims of crime. They are also at high risk for drug and alcohol abuse and sexual situations.

Most of the children who are out late at night, unsupervised by responsible adults, are temperamentally difficult children who don't abide by parents rules, who have lied to their parents about their whereabouts, or whose parents have freed them from adult supervision. The later children stay out at night without supervision the more likely they are to associate with a community's worst-behaved, least-supervised kids. And the more time children spend with these kids, the more likely they are to emotionally bond with them and take on their characteristics, values, and behavior patterns.

Some children are allowed to stay out late at night because temperamentally passive parents, despite wanting their children home, don't know how to stand up to aggressive, argumentative children. Many of these parents simply need a backup to give them the support they need. And a community-wide curfew is all the support many parents need to tell their children to be home at a reasonable time.

Every city needs to consistently enforce a late-night street curfew for those under eighteen years old. Children fourteen years old or older can attend school dances. They can watch movies in a theater, skate at a skating rink, or bowl at a bowling alley undisturbed. But they can't cruise or hang out. Many cities also need daytime truancy patrols to make sure children are at school.

SCHOOLS

Public schools once provided an authoritative, well-structured environment. Most had strict dress and grooming codes; some even required uniforms. Closed campuses were the norm. Hall monitors checked passes to make sure students were out of class legitimately, and students were not allowed to use bad language in or out of class. Parents were notified immediately if their children left school without permission. Parents were also notified promptly if children were having difficulties at school, and in many schools students were required to repeat failed assignments and make up missed work. This needs to be the norm again, and every parent should push schools to reestablish adult authority.

The school day needs to be extended to correspond to the normal work day. In most families no one is at home when the children return from school. As a result, millions of children, especially those over twelve years old, are put at risk every day.

The school year also needs to be lengthened to provide structured, well-supervised summers for children whose parents are at work all day.

Parents as the Solution to Crime and Violence

Every year thousands of crimes, including crimes of violence, are committed by this nation's children, many of whom are gangsters. These children cost the country billions of dollars a year in direct costs and billions more in indirect costs. Many of them will grow up to be adult criminals and gangsters, costing the country tens of billions of dollars during their lifetimes while inflicting untold pain and suffering on their victims. And virtually nothing being done currently is slowing the process. In fact, violent youth crime and gangsterism continue to grow more and more out of control.

The only really good thing to come out of all the projects heretofore set up to curb serious youth crime and gang violence is that we have all learned what doesn't work. In general:

- Delinquents and gangsters refuse to be educated or lectured out of crime and violence.
- Delinquents and gangsters refuse to be counseled out of crime and violence.
- Delinquents and gangsters refuse to be diverted out of crime and violence.
- Delinquents and gangsters refuse to be scared out of crime and violence.
- Delinquents and gangsters refuse to be punished out of crime and violence.
- Delinquents and gangsters refuse to be rewarded out of crime and violence.
- Delinquents and gangsters refuse to let prison keep them away from crime and violence.

Hiring more police officers won't help much to stop youth crime and violence. Building more institutions hasn't helped yet and isn't likely to in the future. And employing more therapists, social workers, and drug and alcohol counselors to work with young criminals and gangsters will be a waste of money.

But there is an answer to the problem of youth violence and gangsterism. It won't cost the country a cent. And, best of all, it can immediately and dramatically reduce youth crime, violence, and gangsterism to low levels. The answer to youth crime of all kinds is putting *parents in control*.

While some parents of young criminals and gangsters are truly dysfunctional and of no use to their children, the majority of parents whose children are involved in gangs and crime are competent enough to take control of their children. They may not know how to discipline and supervise their children. Some may not even want to bother to discipline and supervise their children. But most, with training and continuing emotional support, can and will take control of their children's criminal behavior if the probation department and juvenile court require them to do so. In other words, we must train, support, assist, and rely on parents to do a job that no one else has the time or inclination to do: discipline and supervise their children. And the only agencies with the legal authority to do it are those under the jurisdiction of the nation's juvenile courts. Described below is a program every community can set up to immediately take control of youth crime and violence. This plan gives parents the authority to discipline and supervise their children, with court support, and the responsibility for doing the job right.

PARENT IN CONTROL

1. Parent training classes (ten-week minimum) to teach parents authoritative methods of discipline and supervision.

   a. Authoritative parent training classes should be available to all parents who voluntarily ask for help with out-of-control children, even if the children have not yet committed a crime. It is imperative that we help parents who have recognized that they have a problem controlling their children's behavior, and we must help them as soon as possible rather than waiting until those children victimize someone.

   b. Authoritative parent training classes should be available to all parents referred to the program by a school because of children's misbehavior. Apart from parents, teachers are the first to see serious behavior problems in children.

   c. Authoritative parent training classes should be available to all parents referred to the program by local police agencies. Voluntary referrals should be given to parents whenever a child has been arrested for criminal behavior, even if a petition has been submitted to the probation department.

   d. Authoritative parent training classes should be available to all parents referred to the program by county probation officers. Referrals should be made for the families whose children have been placed on informal probation during the intake process. Referrals should also be made for all existing cases on field supervision caseloads, including gang-suppression units.

   e. Authoritative parent training classes should be required of all parents and probationers ordered by the juvenile court to successfully complete the program.

2. Training classes to teach authoritative methods of discipline and supervision should be required for probation officers, social workers, and anyone else who works with families with out-of-control children. For program consistency and continuity, it is vital that probation officers and others working with the program fully understand what parents are doing and why they are doing it.

3. Establishing the parent-probation team.

   a. In addition to other terms and conditions of probation, children on formal probation for criminal behavior would be required by court order to go to school every school day and to attend all classes on time unless excused for a valid reason by a probation officer.

   b. Children on formal probation for criminal behavior would be required to observe an early curfew: 6:00 P.M. is recommended for most probationers, but an earlier curfew may be appropriate for some potentially dangerous probationers.

   c. Parents with children on formal probation for criminal behavior would be required by court order to immediately notify the probation department if their children fail to go to school or stay out past 6:00 P.M.

   d. All parents and juvenile probationers who violate the above orders will be immediately referred to the juvenile court for possible contempt proceedings. Small to moderate fines or community service sentences should be imposed on parents found in contempt of court. It is imperative that no martyrs be created in this process.

   e. A probation team working in conjunction with the local police would enforce both the curfew and school attendance orders.

4. Outcome of program.

   a. By the end of the ten-week parenting program, participating parents will know how to discipline and supervise their children. They will have learned how to clearly formulate and state household rules, how to enforce those rules without punishment, and how to avoid situations that can lead to family violence. And having learned how to supervise and monitor their children's activities, they will also know how to protect the children from drug and alcohol abuse, school failure, dropping out, and most important, crime and gangs, including gang membership.

b. Because of the external assistance from the probation team, most parents and most out-of-control children will develop new habit patterns that will greatly reduce the likelihood of new criminal behavior or involvement in gang activities. If nothing else, this new approach will keep almost all of the nation's most dangerous young criminals at home at night and at school during the day for the duration of their probation.

The Parents in Control approach to stopping gang involvement and violent crime has to be conducted in a way that supports parents, even those parents who may have to be referred to the juvenile court. The minute an approach becomes punitive in nature—something a number of communities have unsuccessfully tried—it will backfire. Parents have to be made to feel that they are the most important people in their children's lives, which they obviously are, and that the rest of us are here to help them be the best parents they can be.

APPENDIX

§

Questions and Answers

RIGHT AND WRONG

Q. I teach my children right from wrong. Why isn't that enough?

A. Right and wrong are broad intellectual concepts that lack any specificity, structure, rules, or definitions. Human beings learn to behave right through the consistent application of well-defined, specific rules of behavior, not by being told types of behavior are right and others are wrong. Children aren't taught to clean their rooms by being told that it's wrong to have a dirty room. They learn to clean their rooms by having their parents clearly describe the tasks they are to do and then monitor their progress to make sure they are properly done. Nor are children taught to be home on time by parents telling them it's wrong to be late. Children learn to be home on time when parents specify the time they are to be home, consistently monitor their whereabouts for compliance, and, if they are late, immediately bring them home and temporarily restrict their freedom to go out. Learning right from wrong is part of a long, arduous process of structuring the specific rules learned at home, school, work, and elsewhere into a person's overall value system.

PEERS

Q. Don't my children have a right to choose their own friends?

A. No, not exclusively. Who your children spend their time with in large part determines their attitudes, values, and behavior patterns. The most potentially dangerous (or helpful) people your children are ever going to associate with are their friends. Few children use drugs by themselves. Few children get drunk by themselves. Few children are in one-person gangs. Children cannot get pregnant by themselves. And few children commit crime by themselves. If parents don't monitor their children's selection of friends, associates, potential suitors, and sex partners they place their children at high risk for dangerous and destructive behavior.

Q. My sixteen-year-old says he wants to get out of the gang he's been involved with for the last two years, but the other kids won't let him out alive. He said he was "jumped in" and can't get out unless he is "jumped out." Is he lying to me?

A. Yes and no. If he simply stops participating in gang activities, nothing is likely to happen to him, especially if he is willing to be considered a mama's boy and to tell anyone who asks that "My mother [or father] won't let me." If, however, your son openly rejects his fellow gang members and tells them that he is leaving the gang, they may attack him. A little common sense is called for in this situation.

Q. My son, who doesn't get into trouble, wants to participate in neighborhood sports and activity programs for at-risk kids. Should I let him?

A. Not unless you go, too. Without strong adults to consistently supervise them, at-risk children, including young criminals and gangsters, will continue to do as they please, even when they are at a playground, community center, or neighborhood basketball court. Worse yet, there is a continuing process of recruiting new children into criminal and gang subcultures. If you aren't consistently there to protect him, your son will be at risk of bonding with one or more of the delinquents or gangsters playing with him.

In general, you are better off making sure your son plays sports or participates in school, church, or community activities with other low-risk or no-risk kids. Bonding with other well-behaved, well-supervised children will help your son further reinforce and habituate the values and rules you have brought him up to believe in.

But if you are determined to go out of your way to help the at-risk children in your neighborhood and if you wish to include your son, go ahead and volunteer to be a coach or an adviser so you can always be there to supervise. With that level of supervision and structure, your son will probably be okay. If he does start to emotionally bond to dangerous children, you will be there to immediately sever the relationship.

DRUGS, ALCOHOL, AND TOBACCO

Q.   Since they're going to do what they want anyway, isn't it better for children to drink, smoke, or use drugs at home with parents than to do so with strangers?

A.   The problem with this question is that it assumes parents can't adequately supervise their children. It is typically asked by parents who were not well supervised as children and who have no idea how to supervise their own children. Good supervision includes giving children, regardless of their age, only as much freedom as they prove they can handle, and knowing and approving of where their children are, who they are with, and what they are doing.

As to whether parents should drink, smoke, and do drugs with their children, no, they shouldn't—unless they want to give their children tacit approval to drink, smoke, and do drugs.

Q.   I don't really want my teenage daughter to smoke, but of all the things parents have to watch out for, smoking seems like a minor vice. Shouldn't I prioritize the rules I want her to obey and concentrate on enforcing the most important ones?

A.   Yes, you should prioritize the enforcement of your rules. But stopping your daughter from smoking should be high on the list of prohibitions, not just because smoking is unhealthy but also because it is a gateway behavior associated with serious drug and alcohol abuse, early sexual activity, truancy, and dropping out of school. Smoking also serves as an identity badge for high-risk kids to identify one another. Even if your daughter isn't misbehaving, many high-risk kids will be drawn to her because she smokes. And the more she associates with poorly supervised children, the greater the risk that she will be socialized into joining their destructive and dangerous behavior.

TELEVISION, MOVIES, AND MUSIC

Q.   Should I be concerned about the kind of music my children buy and listen to on the radio?

A.   Yes. Very much so. Many children emotionally bond with members of specific bands, with a whole style of music such as gangster rap, heavy metal, or punk, or with peer cliques that are heavily influenced by the public ethos of their favorite bands. It is typical for some of those children to copy the hair, clothing, and jewelry styles of those bands and to take on their values, attitudes, and actions. If a band in its music, videos, or publicity, advocates drugs, drunkenness, violence, or crime, children who share an emotional bond with the band will tend to support and advocate those same values.

Television, however, is a different story. Teenagers and preteens rarely bond with television or movie characters as they do with popular musicians. And even if they did, the lead characters on most television series, unlike many popular musicians, are rarely corrupt, violent, or drug users, and the violence they do use is generally on the side of truth and justice.

Q.   Should I be concerned about the amount of violence my children watch on television?

A.   Not particularly. Some research has found slight situational increases in copycat violence after boys under ten years old have watched violent television programs or movies, but no one has been able to link street or family violence with Saturday morning cartoons, with HBO's violent Thursday nights, or with any other television programs.

Children's violence is developed, nurtured, and habituated through a combination of temperament and training. Many children are born temperamentally aggressive and learn early on to use physically intimidating behavior to get their way. In other families, anger, inconsistency, and chaos tend to produce high levels of violence for everyone, including children. But most street violence involving children is learned and encouraged when children emotionally bond to unsupervised corrupt peer cultures. And the more time children spend with violent peers, the more likely it becomes that violence will play a prominent part in their lives.

CONTROLLING PARENTS

Q. My daughter's therapist says that my daughter is misbehaving because I am too controlling. What does that mean?

A. Well, it could mean that you are paying a lot of money to a therapist who is philosophically committed to undercutting your authority with a so-called democratic parenting treatment model based on compromise and negotiation. Or it could mean you're promoting a continuing power struggle between yourself and your daughter. If it's the former, you may need to find a therapist who will support your authority to set and enforce rules for your children. If it's the latter, you probably have lost sight of your rules and focused on your daughter as the problem. Rules must have purpose. If your rules serve no purpose other than to get children to obey you, all you will produce is anger, frustration, and sometimes violence. To get out of power struggles with children always stay focused on the rules rather than the persons involved: "Take out all of the trash now," not "Why can't I ever count on you to do your chores?" If you can't honestly find a purpose in some of the rules that you want your children to obey, then drop them.

ADOPTION AND FOSTER CARE ISSUES

Q. Open adoptions, where the birth mother or both birth parents are involved in the adopted child's life with the adopted parents, are becoming more common. How well do open adoptions work?

A. The only family arrangement worse for children than an open adoption agreement is a joint physical custody order imposed by a divorce court on a warring couple. The consistency that all children need is constantly threatened when other parties are brought into the home to participate in child-rearing. Even differences between a mother and father in the same home sometimes produce an angry and hostile home environment. Adding other parties, possibly with conflicting values and agendas, to the parenting process can reduce an otherwise good home to chaos and nudge a problem home toward violence. Even though there are bound to be some successful open adoptions, they are at best a crapshoot. Why take the chance with an innocent child for nothing more than a social experiment? After all, there is no evidence that three or four people—including the birth father or the birth mother's other boyfriends or husbands—are better at raising a child than Mom and Dad on their own.

Q. I sent my fifteen-year-old adopted daughter to a private boarding school for out-of-control children. More than half of the other children enrolled at the school are also adopted. Are adopted children more likely to misbehave and get into trouble?

A. Children adopted at birth are slightly more likely to have serious behavior problems than children raised by their birth parents, probably because of an inherited link between impulsive and immature unwed teenage parents and the impulsive and immature children to whom they give birth. But the older the children are before they are finally adopted into a permanent and stable home, the more likely they are to exhibit serious behavior problems, especially if they haven't been placed in a permanent home by the age of three. In general, the greater the level of inconsistency, impermanence, and anger, and the more foster homes the child has been placed in, the higher the risk for all types of dysfunctional behavior.

Fortunately, most older adopted kids will eventually settle down when they are placed in permanent, well-structured, and loving homes, but the more difficult they are, the more time and energy parents must put into building positive habit patterns and loving relationships.

Q. My fourteen-year-old adopted but out-of-control daughter wants to find her birth mother. What do you think of this idea?

A. Not much. Once she is an adult, finished with her schooling, and living a stable life, if she wants your assistance to find her birth mother, help her. But until then, neither of you need the potential interference, frustration, and chaos that could result if she finds her birth mother now. Rarely do such reunions fulfill out-of-control children's expectations or contribute to their emotional well-being. All of the problems that existed before the reunion will continue to fester after it's over, along with any new problems that may be brought in from the birth mother's situation.

Q. My sister-in-law is back in prison and my husband wants to take in her ten-year-old son to raise. He's a cute little boy, and I do feel sorry for him, but I don't trust him. The boy has been in and out of foster care since he was two years old. He was sexually abused, first by one of his mother's boyfriends and then by a boy in foster care. He sets fires, he steals, and he torments both of our little girls whenever he visits our home. He recently asked them if they would "suck him off." How likely is it that we can overcome what he's gone through and turn him around?

A. I am afraid I have only bad news for this boy. Unless other family members are willing to take your husband's nephew into their homes, you and your husband are probably the only chance this boy has to avoid a life of crime and violence. But he is so badly damaged that it would take every bit of time, tenacity, energy, and affection that you could muster, and probably more, to meet his needs. Also, he would be a real threat to your daughters, so I don't think you have a real choice here. Your own children must come first.

Q. Someone anonymously accused my husband and me of child abuse, and the child protection services people took our seven- and eleven-year-old boys and put them in foster care for more than two months. The older boy was in two different homes and the younger one was in three foster homes before the charges were dropped. The eleven-year-old is really pleased to be back home, but his younger brother is distant and belligerent. He has to be told repeatedly to clean up after himself, something that wasn't a problem before they were taken away. How long is this going to last, and is there any way to make things better?

A. Children need stability and consistency in their lives to do well. When children are legally, or illegally, removed from their homes it produces high amounts of stress, anxiety, and fear. To younger children it doesn't make any difference whether the people taking them from their homes and families do so lawfully or not, it is still an unsettling experience. And each time they are moved from receiving home to foster home to another foster home, more stress, anxiety, and fear are produced. Some children take removal from their homes in stride, but others develop serious and long-lasting problems including emotional withdrawal, depression, anger, and defiance.

Your younger son needs a lot of day-to-day consistency, including enforced schedules and routines; personal attention; affection, even if he objects to it; and laughter. Once he feels he can again rely on you to protect him, he will start to rejoin the family. This process can take weeks or months, and sometimes much longer, but given the circumstances you have described, you should have your son back soon.

DECISION MAKING

Q. Shouldn't my children make their own decisions about what to wear?

A. A significant part of your children's identity involves their clothing styles. If you allow them to copy the clothing styles of dangerous and destructive peers, you place them at substantially higher risk of joining that peer clique. So unless you want your children to be identified as gangsters, don't let them dress like gangsters; if you don't want them identified as part of the drug crowd, don't let them dress like drug addicts; and if you don't want them to be identified as "sluts" and "whores"— both words are still popular pejoratives on most junior and senior high school campuses—don't let them dress provocatively.

QUALITY TIME VERSUS QUANTITY TIME

Q. I don't have a lot of time to spend with my children, but the time I do have is quality time. Isn't that good enough?

A. No. Even more important for children than the fun and play periods that normally make up quality time are the boring, mundane, exasperating, and frustrating quantity times when parents monitor homework and chores, stand up to anger and tantrums, and do all of the other things that provide children with a loving, protective structure. There is no substitute, can be no substitute, for the hard work known as quantity time that goes with raising children.

SUPERVISION

Q. If we supervise our children to the extent that you suggest, how will they ever learn to think for themselves?

A. Kids have no problem thinking for themselves. It's their behavior we're concerned about. Your question assumes that human behavior is, in large part, governed by learning from one's mistakes. It isn't. In general, human behavior is governed by impulse, habit, and routine with heavy influences from the people with whom we bond. Generally, children do those things they feel like doing as well as those things they are trained to do by their parents or peers.

The question you asked is often put forth by parents and other adults who don't believe it's their job to supervise the children in their care and who want, at the earliest possible time, to shift the responsibility of children's supervision to the children themselves. This belief is common in America's lowest social classes and fits well in a consequence-based system that relies on children learning to think for themselves because of the punishments they receive.

Unfortunately, the earlier children are released from adult supervision, even if they are consistently and severely punished, the more likely they are to use drugs and alcohol, fail at school, smoke, get pregnant, join gangs, and commit crimes. Children, especially teenagers, need to be supervised at the trust and responsibility levels that their behavior dictates and that the present social climate makes necessary. Normally, parents always need to know and approve of where their children are, what they are doing, and who they are with.

EARLY AND LATE EMANCIPATION

Q. Are there cultural and ethnic differences in child-rearing prac-
    tices that hurt or help children succeed in the United States? If
    so, what are they?

A. Parental supervision is the one significant parenting practice
    that distinguishes how well the children of different ethnic and
    social classes behave. The most significant difference between
    the American social classes identified by sociologists is the age
    at which families start to emancipate their children from paren-
    tal decision-making and supervision. I understand that writing
    critically of social classes and ethnic groups in this age where
    all human groupings have equal value, status, and worth, and
    where no one speaks ill of any group, is socially dangerous. But
    while honoring the value of all individuals is crucial, we must
    also recognize the differences in parenting systems between
    social classes, and between ethnic groups. This is essential if
    everyone in America is going to get a chance at the level
    playing field.

    In general, the lower the social class, the sooner children are
    required to take care of themselves; the higher the social class,
    the longer parents oversee the structure of children's lives.
    Typically, parents in the underclass are rarely if ever consis-
    tently involved in their children's education, while parents in
    the higher classes oversee their children's education through
    college and beyond. Children raised on the bottom rungs of the
    social class structure are freed to make adult decisions regard-
    ing dating, boyfriend and girlfriend relationships, and sex at an
    early age. They are also given adult decision-making authority
    regarding their education, employment, and peer relation-
    ships, with parents rarely doing more than giving advice or
    instruction. Children raised on the higher rungs of the social
    class structure typically find heavy and long-lasting parental
    involvement in most aspects of their daily lives, including a
    high degree of supervision.

    As with the distinction between social classes, one of the
    most important differences in child-rearing practices between
    ethnic groups is the age at which families start emancipating
    children from parental decision-making and supervision. As in

America's social classes, there is a direct relationship in how well children behave at home, school, and in the neighborhood, and when parents free them to make their own decisions. Those ethnic groups with the longest and highest levels of direct parental involvement and supervision tend to produce the best educated, most chaste, and least delinquent children. And, as might be expected, those ethnic groups that emancipate their children earliest tend to have the worst educated, most sexually active, and most delinquent children.

Emancipating children doesn't mean that parents do nothing when they disapprove of their children's behavior. And it certainly doesn't mean they give their children permission to misbehave or to do as they please. They may be upset and angry; they may complain, yell, lecture, nag, throw tantrums, make threats, dump guilt, or castigate their children on daytime television; but for the most part they don't enforce rules. More important, they no longer believe they have the parental duty to make their emancipated children behave ("You can't keep them chained forever").

One of the most successful ways America can stop crime, reduce alcohol and drug abuse, improve school achievement, and maximize life success is to help, encourage, and train parents to maintain control of their children's behavior, as necessary, until they are at least eighteen years old, and then hold them accountable for doing so.

ADULT CHILDREN

Q. Although he is legally an adult, my eighteen-year-old son is very immature and impulsive. He didn't graduate from high school, and he hasn't been able to keep a job for more than two or three weeks at a time. He was recently arrested for shoplifting. He lacks good judgment and is unable to take care of himself. What can I do to help him?

A. Not a lot. Give him love and emotional support and, if he asks for it, good advice. But parents of adult children have few, if any, rights to control their children's behavior.

Q. My twenty-six-year-old daughter is a heroin addict. She has been using drugs since she was sixteen and has been in and out of my house since she was nineteen. She has been through every kind of drug treatment program, but she either left early or went back to drugs as soon as she was out. She prostitutes herself and steals to pay for her drugs. I'm taking care of her and her eight-year-old son. I'm the only real mother the boy has ever known, and I've raised him from birth. I have taken enough, and I want her out of my house. But even though she doesn't give a damn about my grandson, she threatens to take him with her if I do kick her out. What can I do?

A. Hire an attorney experienced in family law, and find out exactly where you stand legally. If there is a way for you to do it, obtain a court order appointing you as your grandson's legal guardian as soon as possible. You need to be in charge of what is going on in your own home, and your grandson needs your strength and determination.

BIBLIOGRAPHY

Allen, Jennifer. "Hanging with the Spur Posse," *Rolling Stone*, July 8–July 22, 1993.

Coles, Robert, and Geoffrey Stokes. *Sex and the American Teenager*. New York: Rolling Stone Press, New York, 1985.

Dash, Leon. *When Children Want Children, The Urban Crisis of Teenage Childbearing*. New York: Morrow, 1989.

Dinkmeyer, Don, and Gary D. McKay. *The Parent's Handbook: Systematic Training for Effective Parenting (STEP)*. Circle Pines: American Guidance Service, 1982.

Dreikurs, Rudolf. *Coping with Children's Misbehavior*. New York: Hawthorn Books, 1972.

Dryfoos Joy. *Adolescents at Risk*. New York: Oxford University Press, 1990.

Egan, Gerard. *A Systematic Approach to Effective Helping*. 4th ed. Pacific Grove, Calif.: Brooks/Cole Publishing, 1990.

Engler, Jack, and Daniel Goleman. *The Consumer's Guide to Psychotherapy*. New York: Simon & Schuster, 1992.

"For Some, Youthful Courting Has Become a Game of Abuse," *New York Times*, July 11, 1993, p. 1.

Gordon, Thomas. *Parent Effectiveness Training: The No-Lose Program for Raising Responsible Children*. New York: Wyden, 1970.

Hippler, A. E. *Hunter's Point: A Black Ghetto*. New York: Basic Books, 1974.

Holt, John. *How Children Fail*. New York: Dell, 1964.

Love, John F. *McDonald's: Behind the Arches*. New York: Bantam Books, 1986.

Mason, Daniel. *Double Duty: Parenting Our Kids While Reparenting Ourselves*. Tucson: Comp Care Publishers, 1990.

Mathews, Anne. "The Ivory Tower Becomes an Armed Camp," *New York Times Magazine*, March 7, 1993.

Padian, Nancy, et al. "Male to Female Transmission of Human Immunodeficiency Virus," *Journal of the American Medical Association* 14 (August 1987): 525–26.

Richards, Dinah. *Has Sex Education Failed Our Teenagers?* Pomona, Calif.: Focus on the Family Publishing, 1990.

Shaw, Clifford R., and Henry D. McKay. *Juvenile Delinquency and Urban Areas.* Rev. ed. Chicago: University of Chicago Press, 1969.

Wexler, Richard. *Wounded Innocents: The Real Victims of the War Against Child Abuse.* Buffalo, N.Y.: Prometheus Books, 1990.

For information about Parent in Control or Back in Control programs, please call (503) 590-9110.

INDEX

abortions, 147
abuse:
  spousal, 18, 73
  see also child abuse
A-category kids, 41, 42
activities, 43, 82–83, 84, 114, 115,
    124–25
  as bonding experiences, 142
  parents' involvement in, 142
adoption, 167–69
  behavior problems and, 168
  open, 167–68
  searching for birth mother
    after, 168–69
adult children, 173–74
affection:
  expressions of, 44, 142
  see also emotional attachment
age:
  of emancipation from
    supervision, 172–73
  trust or freedom and, 85
aggressive behavior, 102
  attention deficit disorder and,
    27–28
  behavioral templates and, 37
  of temperamentally difficult
    children, 23, 24, 26, 37
  see also violent behavior
AIDS, HIV infection and, 99–100,
    127–28
Alanon, 19

alarms, to keep child in house,
    42, 119, 137
alcohol, 18–19, 40, 42, 44, 54,
    102–7, 150, 152–53, 155, 156
    158, 164, 171
  allowing child to experiment
    with, 145–46, 147
  behavioral templates and, 36,
    37
  on college and university
    campuses, 81–82
  democratic parenting therapy
    and, 97
  drinking at home with parents
    165
  preventing use of, 104–5
  sample rules on, 102–3
  sexual activity and, 127, 131
  stopping use of, 105–7, 135–36
  supervision and risk for, 77,
    80–81, 82–83, 104–5
American Civil Liberties Union
    (ACLU), 149
amusement parks, 105
anal sex, 127, 128, 130
anger, 24, 35, 62, 168
  chaotic environment and, 55
  effects of, 143
  inconsistently enforced rules
    and, 39, 46
  temper tantrums and, 72–73
arguing, 63–69

arguing (*cont'd*)
  deflection of, 63–69, 70–71
  reasoning or lecturing and, 93, 94
  sponging and, 63, 67, 69, 71
  about telling the truth, 70–71
  temper tantrums and, 72–73
  threats and, 71–72
Aristotle, 11
assignment books, 121, 123
at-risk children, programs for, 164–65
attachment, *see* emotional attachment
attention deficit disorder (ADD), 26–28, 124
  criminality or violence and, 26–27
  diagnosis of, 27
  with hyperactivity syndrome (ADDHS), 27, 28
  medication and, 27–28
authoritative parent training classes, 159
authority:
  adult, weakening of, 143–54
  see also parental authority

Back in Control Centers, 15, 105
Back in Control Parenting Workshops, 102
  children required to attend, 136–37
badgering, 46, 65–67
bad habits, 29–30
bathroom chores, 24
  sample rules on, 110–11
B-category kids, 41, 42, 114
bear hugs, for smaller violent child, 74–75

bedrooms:
  cleaning or tidying of, 24, 31, 86–88, 102, 109–10, 163
  monitoring contents of, 106, 114–15
beds:
  changing linens on, 109
  getting child out of, 45
  making of, 108
bed-wetting, 98
behavioral templates, 34–55
  arguing and, 69
  emotional responses and, 36
  habits and, 34–35
  household chores and, 35–36, 108
  monitoring and, 35
  negative peer-culture values and, 77, 80, 81
  school performance and, 35, 124
  structural flaws in, 44–46
  structuring of, 36–44
  of temperamentally difficult children, 37
behavior modification, 98–99
birth control, 78
birth mothers, searching for, 168–169
blacks, put down for "acting white," 36
blame, 60–61
boards of education, 121
bonding, 47
  see also emotional attachment
Bonita:
  before Back in Control, 20–21
  after Back in Control training, 139
bowling alleys, 105

boyfriends or girlfriends, 172
  going steady with, 130
  parents' disapproval of, 50–51
  running away with, 136–38
  see also sexual activity
bullying, 24

C-category kids, 42, 113, 114, 117
chaos, 30, 108
  children raised in environment
    of, 53–55
  ethological milieus and, 29
child abuse, 68
  criminality and, 25–26
  mandatory reporting and, 150–
    152
  physical punishment and, 88,
    151–52
  provoked by temperamentally
    difficult children, 26
Child Abuse Prevention and
    Treatment Act (1974), 150–51
child-based cultures, *see* youth
    cultures
children:
  adult, 173–74
  badly structured, 33
  marginally structured, 32
  out-of-control, *see* out-of-
    control children
  parents' emotional attachment
    to, 37–38, 43–44, 91, 142–43,
    146
  rights of, 106, 144, 147, 163–64
  temperamentally difficult, *see*
    temperamentally difficult
    children
  viewing as problem, 60–61
  well-structured, 32
  see also specific topics

child welfare services, 89
chores, *see* household chores
clothes, 31
  associated with gangs,
    delinquent subcultures, and
    criminal peer cliques, 77, 81,
    113, 114, 134, 166
  caring for, 63–65, 109
  child's identity and, 170
  monitoring of, 77
  psychiatric hospital programs
    and, 152
  school dress codes and, 120,
    148, 149, 157
college administrators,
    supervision role refused by,
    84–85
college campuses, crime on, 81–
    82
compromising, 94–95
condoms, 99–100, 127–31, 147
Congress, U.S., 149–50
consequences, allowing child to
    experience, 97–98
consistency, 39–40, 45–46, 115–
    116, 119, 142
  in enforcing chore schedules,
    112
  foster care and, 169–70
  open adoption and, 167–68
  schoolwork and, 122, 125
  see also inconsistency
contracting systems, 14, 98
control, regaining of, 101–32
  over alcohol, drugs, tobacco,
    and crime, 102–7
  first steps in, 101–2
  over gangs, delinquent
    subcultures, and criminal
    peer cliques, 112–16

control, regaining of (*cont'd*)
   over household chores, 107–12
   over running away, 116–19
   over school problems, 119–25
   over sexual activity, 125–32
control, sought by
      temperamentally difficult
      children, 62
controlling behavior, ascribed to
   parents, 167
counseling, *see* psychiatric or
   psychological counseling
court system, *see* juvenile courts
criminality, 15, 40, 42, 44, 54, 81–
   82, 102–7, 153, 164, 171
   abuse as child and, 25–26
   attention deficit disorder and,
     26–27
   behavioral templates and, 37
   household chores and, 36
   ineffective approaches to, 158
   parent battering and, 73
   parents as solution to, 157–61
   sample rules on, 102–3
   supervision and risk for, 83, 104
criminal peer cliques, 112–16
   getting kids out of, 112, 114–16
   preventing involvement with,
     113–14
   sample rules on, 112–13
   see also gangs; peer cliques
criticism, personal, 60–61
curfews, 94–95, 98, 163
   community-wide, 149, 153,
     156–57
   probation and, 160
custody, joint, 50–53

daily planners, 121, 123
Dash, Leon, 78, 126–27

dating, 50–51, 130, 131–32, 172
   see also boyfriends or
     girlfriends
deflection of arguments, 63–69
   about lying, 70–71
   threats and, 71–72
delinquent subcultures, 112–16,
   120
   getting kids out of, 112, 114–16
   preventing involvement with,
     113–14
   sample rules on, 112–13
   see also gangs; peer cliques
democratic parenting therapy, 97,
   167
desire, acting on, 23–24
Detroit, screening for weapons in
   schools of, 149
Dinkmeyer, Don, 97, 144, 145, 146
discipline, 37–40, 86, 90
   clearly defined and stated rules
     needed in, 38
   consistency needed in, 39–40,
     45–55
   flawed, examples of, 46–55
   follow-through and monitoring
     in, 38–39, 45, 46
   requiring of parents, 158–61
   structural flaws and, 44–55
Disneyland, 105
divorce, joint custody and, 50–53
Dreikers, Rudolf, 98
dress codes, 120, 148, 149, 157
drugs, 40, 42, 44, 54, 81, 82, 102–
   107, 114, 150, 152–53, 155,
   156, 158, 164, 171
   adult child's use of, 173–74
   allowing child to experiment
     with, 145–46, 147
   behavioral templates and, 36, 37

democratic parenting therapy
   and, 97
educating children about, 99
preventing use of, 104–5
psychiatric hospital programs
   and, 152
sample rules on, 102–3
sexual activity and, 127, 131
stopping use of, 105–7
supervision and risk for, 77, 80,
   82–83, 104–7
using at home with parents,
   165
dusting, 109

eating, behavioral templates and,
   34
Eddy:
   before Back in Control, 18–19
   after Back in Control training,
      135–36
education:
   as means of controlling
      misbehavior, 99–100
   parental oversight of, 172
   see also schools and schoolwork
emotional attachment, 37–38, 43–
   44, 91, 142–43, 146
emotionally based behavior, 23–
   24, 30–32, 76, 100
   behavioral templates and, 36
   logic and reasoning ineffective
      with, 92–94
enforcement:
   consistent, see consistency;
      inconsistency
   methods of, 42–43
   see also monitoring
ethnic groups, parenting
   differences and, 172–73

ethological milieus, 29, 76
   in inner cities, 78–79, 126
   potentially dangerous and
      corrupting, 40–41; see also
      gangs; peer cliques
   regaining control and, 106,
      107
   of street kids, 116

failure, freedom-to-fail approach
   and, 14, 120, 146, 147–48
fire-escape plans, 42, 119, 137
follow-through, 38–39, 45, 46
   household chores and, 111–12
footwear, 81, 113, 114
   caring for, 109
Ford, Gerald, 149–50
foster children, 168, 169–70
   sexual activity of, 126, 127
freedom-to-fail approach, 14, 120,
   146, 147–48
friends:
   children's right to choose, 163–
      164
   see also boyfriends or
      girlfriends; peer cliques;
      peers

Galt decision, 150
gangs, 37, 40, 42, 76, 101, 102,
   112–16, 120, 148, 171
   getting child out of, 112, 114–
      116, 133–34, 164
   ineffective approaches to, 158
   parents as solution to, 157–
      161
   preventing involvement with,
      113–14
   rap and, 81
   sample rules on, 112–13

gangs (*cont'd*)
  supervision and risk for, 83, 113–16
  see also peer cliques
gangster rap, 81, 166
gay men, sexual activity of, 127–128
Genovese, Eugene D., 79
girlfriends, *see* boyfriends or girlfriends
girls:
  boys showing disrespect to, 79
  teen pregnancy and, 37, 44, 78, 139, 152–53, 168, 171
going steady, 130
Gordon, Thomas, 144–45, 146
graffiti taggers, 101, 113, 114–115
grandparents, 28, 122, 155, 174
group homes, sexual activity in, 126
Guns N' Roses, 81

habits:
  bad, 29–30
  behavioral templates and, 34–35
hairstyles, 77, 81, 113, 114, 166
hall monitors, 157
heavy metal, 81, 82, 101, 113, 166
heredity, 168
Hippler, Arthur, 79
HIV, 99–100, 127–28
HMOs, counseling at, 22
Holt, John, 144, 147
homelessness, 54, 150
home schooling, 122
homework, *see* schools and schoolwork
hospital programs, 14

house, locking child in, 42–43, 119, 135–36, 137
household chores, 30, 107–12
  attention deficit disorder and, 27, 28
  behavioral templates and, 35–36, 108
  as bonding experiences, 142
  chaotic environment and, 53–55
  consistency in enforcing schedules for, 112
  focusing on child as problem and, 60–61
  gender factors and, 35
  mental health models and, 98
  monitoring and follow-through of, 111–12
  nagging about, 35, 47–48, 57–58, 60–61
  parent-child attachment and, 44
  prioritizing of misbehavior and, 102, 107
  punishment for not doing, 86–89
  results of structuring and, 32–33
  sample rules on, 108
  setting schedule for, 57–58, 59–60, 108, 112
  specific job descriptions for, 56–59, 108–11
  specifying who is to do, 60
  supervision and, 84, 111–12
  temperamentally difficult children and, 24, 25, 107
Hunter's Point (San Francisco), 79

hyperactivity syndrome, attention deficit disorder with (ADDHS), 27, 28

impulsiveness, 93, 168
    attention deficit disorder and, 26–28
    behavioral templates and, 37
    parents' control of, 26
    of temperamentally difficult children, 23–24, 25, 29–32, 37, 76
inconsistency, 46–55, 108, 168
    chaotic environment and, 53–55
    effects of, 39–40, 46–55, 142
    joint custody and, 50–53
    nagging and, 47–48
    parental conflict and, 49–50
    rescuers and, 48–49
    see also consistency
inner cities, 126, 153, 155
    children raising children in, 78–79, 85
insensitivity, 23, 25
interests:
    encouraging of, 43
    see also activities
"I" statements, 61

jails, visits to, 96–97
Jason:
    before Back in Control, 17–18
    after Back in Control training, 133–34
jewelry, 81, 113, 114, 166
job descriptions:
    in business world, 58
    sample, for household chores, 108–11
    specific, need for, 56–59

joint custody, 50–53
Journal of the American Medical Association, 127
Julie:
    before Back in Control, 19–20
    after Back in Control training, 136–38
juvenile courts, 15, 18, 74, 155–156
    in enforcement of parental responsibility, 158–61
    limits on authority of, 149–50, 152, 153
    mandatory rules in, 45–46
juvenile halls, 133–34
    sexual activity in, 126
    visits to, 96–97
Juvenile Justice Act (1974), 149–150, 152, 153

killing, 81
kitchen, chores in, 24, 47–48, 53–54, 91
Knott's Berry Farm, 105

latchkey children, 85, 157
laundry, 109, 110
learning disabilities, 36, 124
lecturing, 92–94
literal interpretations, of rules, 56–57
locks, to keep child in house, 42–43, 119, 135–36, 137
logic, 23–24, 92–94
Los Angeles Times Magazine, 127–128
love, 86
    expressions of, 142
    inconsistently given, 47
    see also emotional attachment

lunchtime, students allowed to leave campus during, 19
lying, 42, 70–71

McDonald's, 58
machismo, 18
McKay, Gary, 97, 144, 145, 146
McKay, Henry, 80
makeup, 31, 48–49
malls, hanging out in, 114
manipulation, 62
   lying and, 70–71
   temper tantrums and, 72–73
marriage problems, 50
Mason, Daniel, 145–46, 147
mediating, 98
medication, attention deficit disorder and, 27–28
mentally ill, 54
   released from state hospitals, 149–50
Metallica, 81
minimal literalism, 56–57
misbehavior, 13–14, 23–33
   attention deficit disorder and, 26–28
   covering up with lie, 70–71
   emotional logic of, 30–32
   experiencing natural consequences of, 97–98
   ineffective methods of control and, 86–100
   prioritizing of, 102, 107
   structural flaws and, 44–55
   temperamentally difficult children and, 23–26
   see also alcohol; criminality; drugs; gangs; running away, runaways; sexual activity; tobacco; violent behavior

monitoring, 38–39, 45, 46, 143, 163, 164
   of household chores, 111–12
   to regain control over alcohol, drugs, tobacco, or criminality, 105–7
   see also supervision
mothers:
   abused by spouse, 18, 73
   birth, searching for, 168–69
   undermined by machismo, 18
   unwed, 78, 81, 139, 168
   see also parents
motion-sensor alarms, 42, 119, 137
motor skill development, 21, 36
movies, 105, 166
music:
   monitoring preferences in, 77, 114, 166
   youth-culture icons and, 81, 113, 166

nagging, 35, 47–48, 57–58, 60–61, 143
natural and logical consequences model, 97–98
"nevertheless," deflection technique and, 63–69
New York Times, 79
Nicole:
   before Back in Control, 21–22
   after Back in Control training, 140–41
nightclubs, teenage, 105, 117
nose picking, 98
N.W.A. (Niggers With Attitude), 81

organizational skills, behavioral templates and, 35

out-of-control children:
  attention deficit disorder and,
    26–28
  case studies of, 17–22, 133–41
  locking in house, 42–43, 119,
    135–36, 137
  medication of, 27–28
  misbehavior of, 13–14, 23–33;
    see also alcohol; criminality;
    drugs; gangs; running away,
    runaways; sexual activity;
    tobacco; violent behavior
  provocation and manipulation
    tactics of, 62–75
  regaining control of, 101–32
  temperamentally difficult, see
    temperamentally difficult
    children

parental authority:
  child-abuse laws and, 150–52
  education system and, 147–49
  juvenile courts and, 74
  mental health models and, 97–
    98, 144, 167
  parenting professionals'
    antiauthoritarianism and,
    97–98, 144–47
  restoring of, 155–56
  over sexual issues, 147
  supposed ineffectiveness of,
    145
  weakening of, 13, 14, 144–54
parental conflict, inconsistency
  and, 49–50
Parent Effectiveness Training
  (P.E.T.), 61, 144–45
parenting professionals, 14
  antiauthoritarianism of, 97–98,
    144–47

see also psychiatric or
  psychological counseling
parenting programs, 14
parents:
  authoritative training classes
    for, 159
  child's emotional attachment
    to, 37–38, 43–44, 91, 142–43,
    146
  informal support networks for,
    155
  institutional support for, 149–
    150, 153, 155–56
  literally interpreting words of,
    56–57
  passive, 26, 156
  regaining control over child,
    101–32
  as solution to crime and
    violence, 157–61
  temperamental traits of, 26
  violent behavior toward, 17–
    18, 73–75
parties, 104–5
  unsupervised, 77, 81, 117
passive parents, 156
  aggressive children and, 26
peer cliques, 40–41, 76–77, 79–81,
    82, 85, 101, 102, 112–16, 120,
    166, 170
  behavioral templates and, 77,
    80, 81
  clothing, jewelry, and
    hairstyles associated with,
    77, 81, 113, 114, 134, 166
  getting kids out of, 112, 114–16
  preventing involvement with,
    113–14
  running away and, 116
  sample rules on, 112–13

peer cliques (*cont'd*)
  sexually active, 130
  youth culture icons and, 81,
    113, 166
  see also gangs
peers:
  child's right to choose friends
    and, 163–64
  classification system for, 41–42
  negative, 21, 40–41, 43, 65–67,
    76–77, 79–82, 85, 101, 102,
    105–7, 116, 117, 119, 124, 143,
    164–66, 167
  overseeing associations and
    friendships with, 41, 104
pickup services, for runaways, 118
Planned Parenthood, 147
playgrounds, supervision of, 123
police, 153, 155–56, 158, 159
  enlisting aid of, 133–34
  runaways and, 118
power struggles, 167
pregnancy, 37, 44, 139, 152–53,
    164, 168, 171
  ethological milieu and, 78
principals, 121
prisons, 150
  visits to, 96–97
privacy, child's right to, 106, 144,
    147
probation, 149, 150, 153, 155–56
  in enforcement of parental
    responsibility, 158–61
  school and curfew conditions
    of, 160
probation officers, authoritative
    training classes for, 160
pro-choice advocates, 147
provocation, 62–75
  arguing and, 63–69

inviting child to leave home
    during, 95–96
  threats and, 71–72
  violence and, 73–75
psychiatric centers, 74, 117, 152
psychiatric or psychological
    counseling, 14, 19, 22, 97–99,
    158
  antiauthoritarianism in, 97–98,
    144–47, 167
  behavior modification, 98–99
  contracting model, 98
  democratic parenting therapy,
    97, 167
  mediating model, 98
  natural and logical
    consequences model, 97–
    98
Public Enemy, 81
punishment, 14, 22, 143, 171
  behavior modification and, 98–
    99
  creative, 89
  ineffectiveness of, 86–91, 152
  physical, 88, 151–52
  at school, 89–90
  of temperamentally difficult
    children, 25–26, 90
punks, 81, 82, 101, 113, 166

quality time, quantity time vs.,
    170–71

racism, 31–32
Rahway State Prison, 96
rap, 81, 166
rape, 81, 126, 147
reasoning, 23–24, 92–94
"regardless," deflection
    technique and, 63–69

relationships, inconsistency
damaging to, 40, 142
"release with love," 14, 19
religious programs, 44
rescuers, 48–49
residential treatment programs,
15, 74
sexual activity in, 126
responsibility:
schedules and, 60
temperamentally difficult
children's lack of, 25
trust earned by, 38–39
restraining orders, 138
rewards, 14, 22, 25, 43, 91
behavior modification and, 98–
99
rights of children:
to choose own friends, 163–64
to privacy, 106, 144, 147
right vs. wrong, learning about,
163
rooms, see bedrooms
Rousseau, Jean-Jacques, 144
rules:
on alcohol, drugs, tobacco, and
crime, 102–3
clearly defined and stated, 38,
59, 143, 163
compromising on, 94–95
consistent enforcement of, 29,
39–40, 45–46, 142
ethological milieus and, 29
follow-through and monitoring
of, 38–39, 45, 46
on gangs, delinquent
subcultures, and criminal
peer cliques, 112–13
on household chores, 108
in juvenile courts, 45–46

literal interpretations of, 56–57
mental health models and, 97–
98
missing or poorly defined, 56–
61
power struggles and, 167
prioritizing of, 165
on running away, 117
schedules and, 57, 58, 59–60
on school and schoolwork,
120–21
on sexual activity, 125–26, 128–
130
specific job descriptions and,
56–59
running away, runaways, 15, 19–
20, 42, 44, 101, 102, 107, 116–
119
child's provocations and, 95–
96
finding and picking up, 117–19
prevention of, 117
regaining control over, 136–38
sample rules on, 117
supervision and, 80
support systems for, 116

Scared Straight, 96–97
schedules, 143
for homework, 123–24, 125
for household chores, 57–58,
59–60, 108, 112
schools and schoolwork, 30, 102,
119–25, 153, 156
attention deficit disorder and,
27, 28, 124
behavioral templates and, 35,
124
consistency in parents'
supervision of, 122, 125

schools and schoolwork (*cont'd*)
  defeat and failure in, 21–22,
    171
  democratic parenting therapy
    and, 97
  dress codes in, 120, 148, 149,
    157
  dropping out of, 44, 54, 152, 165
  lack of supervision in, 19, 148
  making rules mandatory in, 46
  monitoring and follow-through
    of, 121–25
  notifying parents about
    problems in, 120, 121, 148,
    157
  with open campuses, 19, 148
  paralleling work day in, 157
  parenting professionals' views
    on, 144–47
  parents' attendance of, with
    misbehaving child, 122–23,
    125
  playground misbehavior in,
    123
  preventing contact with
    negative peers in, 106, 115
  probation and, 160
  punishment in, 89–90
  reestablishing authority in, 157
  results of structuring and, 32–
    33
  reversing poor performance in,
    140–41
  sample rules on, 120–21
  schedules for, 123–24, 125
  sexual activity and, 131
  sudden decline of performance
    in, 80
  supervision and performance
    in, 83
  temperamentally difficult
    children and, 24, 25, 83, 120,
    122, 148
  truancy and, 18, 19–20, 42, 45,
    46, 80, 120, 122, 138, 148, 157,
    165
  undermining of parental
    authority in, 147–49
  well vs. poorly structured,
    119–20
  see also teachers
self-centeredness, 23
self-defense training, 74
sex clubs, 127–28
sexual activity, 20–21, 31, 40, 77,
    93, 125–32, 156, 165, 172
  allowing children to
    experiment with, 145–46, 147
  behavioral templates and, 36,
    37
  condoms and, 99–100, 127–31,
    147
  democratic parenting therapy
    and, 97
  disrespect for girls and, 79–
    80
  educating children about, 99–
    100
  in inner cities, 78, 79
  parental authority over, 145,
    147
  rules on, 125–26, 128–30
  school performance and, 131
  stopping of, 139
  supervision and risk for, 84,
    130–31
sexual harassment, 79, 128, 129–
    130
sexually transmitted diseases,
    99–100, 127–28, 147

sharecropping era, destructive
    child-rearing practices of, 78,
    79
Shaw, Clifford, 80
siblings, 30–31
    comparisons to, 63–64
    hitting of, 70–71
skating rinks, 105
skinheads, 31–32, 76, 81, 82, 101,
    113, 115
slavery era, destructive child-
    rearing practices of, 79
smoke detectors, 42, 119
smoking, see tobacco
social class, parenting differences
    and, 172
social cliques, see peer cliques
social services, 153, 156
    for runaways, 116
social workers, 147, 158
    authoritative training classes
    for, 160
sponging, 63, 67, 69, 71
sports, in programs for at-risk
    children, 164–65
spousal abuse, 18, 73
Spur Posse, 79–80
stealing, 93, 98, 103, 104
    see also criminality
stepparents, 49
structuring, 29–33, 86, 90–91
    of behavioral templates, 36–44
    children's need for, 30–32
    discipline and, 37–40
    ethological milieus and, 29
    flaws in, 44–55
    learning right from wrong and,
    163
    results of, 32–33
    supervision and, 37–38, 40–43

study programs, 22
subcultures:
    delinquent, 112–16
    see also gangs; peer cliques;
    youth cultures
suicide threats, 71–72
superintendents, 121
supervision, 37–38, 40–43, 76–85,
    86, 90–91, 165
    age of emancipation from, 172–
    173
    criminality and, 83, 104–7
    drugs, alcohol, or tobacco and,
    77, 80–81, 82–83, 104–7
    enforcement methods and, 42–
    43
    flawed, effects of, 76–82
    gang affiliation and, 83, 113–
    116
    of impulsive and aggressive
    children, 28
    influence of negative peers
    and, 40–41
    learning to think for oneself
    and, 172
    need for, 84–85
    by other children, 77–79, 85
    peer associations and, 41, 104
    requiring of parents, 158–61
    school performance and, 83,
    119–25
    sexual activity and, 84, 130–
    131
    structural flaws and, 44–55
    work habits or chores and, 84,
    111–12
Supreme Court, U.S., 150
swearing, 68–69
Systematic Training for Effective
    Parenting (S.T.E.P.), 144, 145

Taco Bell, 58

taggers, 101, 113, 114–15

talents, encouraging of, 43

tantrums, *see* temper tantrums

tattoos, 114

teachers, 147
  enlisting cooperation of, 121–122
  freedom-to-fail approach and, 120, 147–48
  in identification of behavior problems, 159
  incompetent or poorly trained, 122–23
  rule enforcement by, 46
  supervision role refused by, 84–85
  talking back to, 121
  see also schools and schoolwork

teen pregnancy, 37, 44, 78, 139, 152–53, 168, 171

telephones, disconnecting of, 137

television, 166

temper, 24, 37, 102

temperament, 34

temperamentally difficult children, 23–26, 152, 153
  aggressive behavior of, 23, 24, 26, 37
  arguing by, 63–69
  behavioral templates of, 37
  capable of being structured into organized, self-disciplined lives, 29–30
  control of situation sought by, 62
  curfews and, 156
  custody arrangements for, 53
  difficult to attach to, 43

emotional logic in misbehavior of, 30–32
  freedom-to-fail approach and, 148
  household chores and, 24, 25, 107
  impulsiveness of, 23–24, 25, 29–32, 37, 76
  logic and reasoning ineffective with, 92–94
  lying by, 70–71
  parents' temperament and, 26
  psychiatric or psychological counseling for, 97–99
  punishment of, 25–26, 90
  reward systems and, 91
  at risk for chemical involvement, 82
  at risk for crime and gang affiliation, 83
  at risk for destructive work habits, 84
  at risk for failure in school, 83
  at risk for sexual activity, 84
  schedules needed by, 60
  school performance of, 24, 25, 83, 120, 122, 148
  sexual activity of, 125, 126, 131
  socially dangerous places and, 40–41
  tantrums of, 72–73
  threats made by, 71–72
  traits of, 23–24, 76
  violent behavior of, 73–75

temperamentally difficult parents, 26

temper tantrums, 18, 25, 72–73, 98
  holding technique for, 74–75, 135–36

time-outs and, 72–73
    violent, 75
therapy, *see* psychiatric or
    psychological counseling
threatening, 71–72
time, quality vs. quantity, 170–71
time-outs, 72–73, 74
tobacco, 42, 102–7, 171
    as gateway drug, 165–66
    preventing use of, 104–5
    psychiatric hospital programs
        and, 152
    sample rules on, 102–3
    stopping use of, 105–7
    supervision and risk for, 80,
        82–83, 104–5
    using at home with parents,
        165
Tough Love, 14
trash, taking out, 47–48, 57–58,
    59–60, 89
    clearly defining rules on, 59,
        109
    setting and enforcing
        schedules for, 59–60
truancy, 18, 19–20, 42, 45, 46, 80,
    120, 122, 138, 165
    notifying parents about, 148
    patrols and, 157
trust, 47, 85, 106
    earned by responsibility, 38–39
tutoring, 124
twelve-step programs, 19

unemployment, chronic, 54
university campuses, crime on,
    81–82

vacuuming, 109–10
vandalization of property, 40, 121
violent behavior, 15, 31–32, 37,
    44, 81, 101, 102, 153
    arguing leading to, 69
    attention deficit disorder and,
        26–27
    habituation of, 166–67
    ineffective approaches to, 158
    toward parents, 17–18, 73–
        75, 102, 133–34
    parents as solution to, 157–
        61
    in schools, 121
    television and, 166
    see also criminality
visitation rights, 52
volunteer work, 43

Washington, D.C.:
    children raising children in,
        78
    curfews for children in, 149
    sexual activity of children in,
        78, 126–27
weapons, 114, 121
Wexler, Richard, 151
*Where There Is a Will There Is an
    "A,"* 22
wife battering, 18, 73
wilderness programs, 15, 74, 102
work habits, supervision and, 84

yard work, 56–57
"you" statements, 60–61
youth cultures, 76–77, 80, 85
    idols and icons of, 81, 113, 166